RACE TO
WIN

RACE TO
WIN

THE 7 ESSENTIAL
SKILLS OF THE
COMPLETE CHAMPION

DEREK DALY

OCTANE
PRESS

Originally published by Motorbooks (Feb. 15, 2008)
under ISBN 978-0-7603-3185-9
Octane Press, Edition 2.0, May 2013
Copyright © 2013 by Derek Daly

ISBN 1-937747-26-3
ISBN-13: 978-1-937747-26-8

Copyedited by Charles Everitt
Proofread by Leah Noel
Interior Design by Diana Boger
Cover Design by Tom Heffron

octanepress.com

Printed in the United States of America

CONTENTS

FOREWORD

BY MARIO ANDRETTI

I'M OFTEN ASKED what it takes to become successful in motor racing. I never know quite what to say, mostly because there is no short answer. I know what it took for me to be successful, but I certainly can't explain it in five minutes—maybe not even five hours. It's just too complex.

So when Derek Daly told me he had written a book on how to become successful in motor racing, I was intrigued. The more I read, the more impressed I became with his effort. The book offers a true driver development path laid out for drivers, team managers and parents to follow.

I was particularly impressed with his Champions Pyramid, which has seven qualities that a driver needs to possess (and balance) to succeed. The more balance, the more success. Every element is there—and it's all important. Like no ingredient in a cake is the most important. Miss one, and the whole cake is ruined.

But I think the most fascinating aspect of the book is the number of anecdotes that Derek uses. He cites real drivers and countless scenarios to make his points—and he didn't make this stuff up. It's an examination and breakdown of drivers that results in valuable insight and coaching. My hope is that in reading this, someone quickly learns a lesson it took guys like me years to learn. Quite honestly, the lessons in this book could resonate far beyond the racing industry.

I believe it takes a focused, systematic approach to become successful in racing today. And Derek's years racing at the highest levels, along with his time observing drivers from the broadcast booth, gave him the frame of reference and expertise needed to clearly articulate the required ingredients to succeed as a race driver. The result is a book that is extremely worthwhile and straightforward. For sure the next time someone asks me what it takes to become a driving champion, I'll have an answer: Read Derek's book.

Mario Andretti

THE PURSUIT OF RACE DRIVER EXCELLENCE

WHEN THE FIRST EDITION of *Race to Win* was published in 2008, it fulfilled a passionate drive for me to capture the essence of driver development between two book covers. As you can imagine, the book was about a subject that is very close to my heart: the development of an elite athlete race car driver. After two printings of the original manuscript, it's time for a second edition. The world has changed a lot since the first manuscript was published and the world of motorsports in particular has changed considerably. When you add the likes of Lewis Hamilton, Sebastian Vettel and Will Power to an already impressive list of driver examples, edition two really packs some horsepower.

I spent most of my adult life immersed in the colorful, glamorous and exciting world of Formula 1, Indy Cars and World Sports Cars, and all this came despite my humble beginnings as the son of a middle-class grocery store owner in Dublin, Ireland.

I won many championships along the way in the lower formulae; however, I never became a champion at the highest levels (ranked 10th in the Formula 1 world championship in 1980), nor did I win an Indy Car race (third place in Milwaukee being the best) or a Grand Prix (although I came very close in Monaco in 1982 when I led on the second last lap only to have the gearbox fail).

While I competed across the globe in Formula 1 from 1978 to 1982, I began to struggle to maintain the form that had been so natural for me in the lower formulae, not unlike many drivers we see today. It was only years afterward that I began to wonder why, and that led me to years of fascinating studies and research to understand why some drivers grew to become successful champions and what the difference really was between good and great. Many will tell you to be successful in anything you have to have qualities such as killer instincts. Well, this book will show you that to become a legendary motorsports champion requires a whole lot more.

One of the reasons I believe I am qualified to write this book is that I was one of the few drivers in the world who got to live his dream of racing at the highest levels in the world, the Formula 1 world championship. Just as it is today, Formula 1 cars in the 1980s were the fastest and most sophisticated cars on the planet. The teams operated at the highest levels of what was known at that time and we traveled the world just as Formula 1 does today. What's different today is the amount of information that's now known. If the world's data doubles every two years (in 2013), just imagine what we know today that we didn't back in the day. Throughout my career in Formula 1 and even into Indy Car racing, I personally made all (or most of) the classic mistakes. I derailed my career many times and had to come back from self-destruction several times. I experienced (although I didn't know it a the time) what I grew to know as "the genesis of self sabotage."

There is nothing like experience to help a driver discover the full effect of his actions, and my experiences, both good and bad, are part of what I want to capture in this book, with the hope that it can direct maybe a few young drivers down the right path to success. I will also use many real life examples of some of the established great drivers in an effort to clearly show that there is no magic bullet when you shoot for success. There is, however, a clear list of ingredients and key moves necessary to become an elite athlete and a complete champion. As you read this book, I want you to see yourself in the examples. I want you to see yourself and the path you might have taken, might be taking, or might be able to take in the future. As you read the different chapters, please remember your ultimate success will be a product of your choices and the choices of those around you. Please also remember that some of the information in this book is somewhat age sensitive, so don't expect your 8-year-old to understand all that is contained herein.

I have spent many years studying the great champions such as Andretti (both Mario and Michael), Schumacher, Vettel, Alonso, Hamilton, Jimmie Johnson and Jeff Gordon. I have asked many probing questions. I have consulted with many professional journalists whose job it is to study and know the athletes, and I now know that there are six key elements necessary for building what I call the Champions Pyramid. They are talent identification, technical ability, communication skills, mental skills, physical skills and on the top is the all important desire and commitment. There are many sub sections within each skill block, but the major building blocks of the Champions Pyramid are key to your understanding of the very foundations of long-term success.

In this, the second edition of this book, I have updated many of the drivers and information, along with turning the Champions Pyramid upside down. Turning the Champions Pyramid upside down has been done for a particular reason. It stands to reason that if you are starting with pretty much nothing, then the first block should be the smallest block. In addition, the upside-down pyramid gives a real feel for the delicate balance that motorsports athletes must now work with, and to show more clearly that you need a holistic and balanced approach. It just screamed at me that the pyramid should be upside down. I think you will find this new approach a refreshing look at what it takes to be the best you can be.

ONE

THE CHAMPION'S PYRAMID BALANCE

The best drivers are the ones who take control of the their environment, develop all the ingredients necessary for success and understand the principals of working with a team.

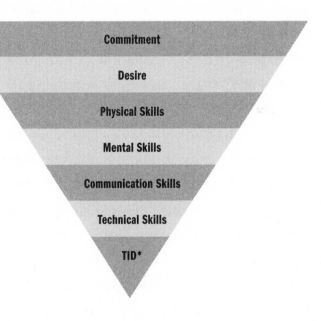

Commitment

Desire

Physical Skills

Mental Skills

Communication Skills

Technical Skills

TID*

*Talent Identification

THROUGHOUT THIS BOOK I will use many analogies and word pictures. The reason I use so many analogies is that most people are visual learners and I want to paint the picture as much as possible. A visual that I think is very important and easy to understand is what I like to refer to as the Champion's Pyramid.

The Champion's Pyramid, which has equal length sides, represents the balance a champion driver needs. The illustration is a simple pictorial description of what a champion is aiming to build. This contradicts the way many have portrayed a pyramid over the years. But there is method to this madness. This book will take you, step by step, to an understanding as to why each element is necessary and how to develop those elements.

As you study the Champion's Pyramid, keep in mind that all through your racing career you are aiming for a balanced triangle. Now, every race and every test session will alter the triangle, because the knowledge and/or experience changes with every lap you do in a race car. In order to have a balanced pyramid and therefore sustainable high performance that will stand the test of time, each element of the pyramid needs to be well developed. And so the upside pyramid reinforces this idea of balance and keeping your development on the razor's edge. If you under- or over-develop any one aspect, the pyramid begins to lean to one side or the other and too much lean equals a topple.

If you have a wealth of technical knowledge for example, but are short on communication and mental skills, your personal pyramid will be unbalanced. The more balanced the package, the more successful you will be and the longer that success will last.

RESEARCH

In 1996, the Derek Daly Academy, led by my former Nissan GTP teammate Bob Earl, created one of the most comprehensive driver development programs in the U.S. It was called the Team Green Academy and was created on behalf of Brown & Williamson (under the KOOL cigarette brand), then a major CART Champ Car sponsor. Bob was a very good driver and an even better teacher/coach. Bob was exceptionally good at creating driving exercises and environments that really stretched drivers. That program gave me direct access to the physical, emotional and mental makeup of almost 50 of the youngest potential stars of American motorsports. It was an eye-opener and a fascinating look into what made some drivers tick, and what derailed them.

What I hear most of all from young drivers is the reasons why they can't do something. No one will pay for the privilege of them racing cars, so they stop. Well maybe they should stop because perhaps they were never going to make it anyway. No matter how much driving talent they have, if they do not possess the desire and commitment to keep going when times get tough, they will fail. There is no real magic to becoming a champion, but you do have to have all the ingredients necessary to be successful and you have to have them aligned more often than your competition. We call this *positioning* a driver for success.

I want this book to show clearly how the best drivers, who more often than their competition *position* themselves for success, are the ones who take control of their environment, develop all six components necessary and understand the principles of working in a team environment. I also want this book to show the most complete drivers in the world were not necessarily born that way, but rather they were developed and trained to be that way.

Throughout the book, you will see I have drawn upon the professional knowledge of many of the world's most respected journalists. They are professionals (and mostly friends of mine) who scrutinize every aspect of the world's greatest race car drivers. Their insights have proven invaluable, as I have gathered the type of illustrative information needed to present the content in this book in the most emotionally engaging way.

EVERY RACE CAR DRIVER IS UNIQUE

Drivers come in many shapes and sizes, and many have been very successful in different eras. It's almost impossible to compare drivers from different eras because of the different equipment and knowledge that was available to them.

Teammates are always compared because they are largely in equal equipment. There is no doubt motorsports has a way of physically and mentally challenging drivers (and team members), and over the years you will find that there is absolutely nowhere to hide in motorsports. You can make excuses all you want, but eventually your weaknesses or differences will become known to so many as to potentially assist your exit from the sport.

Something we have added to this second edition is style difference. Don't confuse different styles for different abilities. Every driver will have his own unique ability and style and that style will suit and not suit some cars and/or tires. At the highest levels we now know different styles can have a great effect on the end result. The more aware a driver is of his style, the more opportunity a driver has to adjust his style if possible. Experience tells us drivers can sometimes adjust their styles, but never really change their natural tendencies.

Two Formula 1 Champions, Lewis Hamilton and Jenson Button, competed as teammates in the same McLaren equipment. Respected journalist Peter Windsor contrasted their different styles in *F1 Racing* magazine in September 2012:

"Jenson (as he has done from the day he first drove a Williams) sculpts an ultra-smooth Jim Russell textbook racing line. His use of throttle and brake—and off throttle against left-foot-brake overlap—is as near-perfect as it can be in a left-foot era. And his feel for throttle-against-loaded-outside-rear is right up there with that of Kimi (when Kimi was at McLaren). He is brilliant, therefore, on long corners; in the wet and from apex to exit on slow corners. And he knows, of course, how to look after a set of tires.

"He has an Alonso-like ability to find subtle moments in which to straighten out the corner, thus enhancing his ability to make quick changes of direction; his unmatched (in this era) feel for the brake pedal in the big stops from high speed; and— as is the case with Fernando—his innate feel for manipulating the car at exactly the right rate and time. Lewis also has softer initial steering and brake input than Fernando—a comparison that isn't really relevant to Jenson because of Jenson's longer, more-rounded corners.

"Lewis is more fearless than Jenson—partly because of the way he drives (Lewis's straighter approach and lower minimum speed provides more scope mid-corner to react to sudden changes in the variables) and partly because of their temperaments: Lewis relishes the concept of having to deal with high-speed flick oversteer (if that is what is comes down to), while Jenson will always try to improve the car if it doesn't feel quite right."

These are two very different styles of driving essentially the same car, and on a certain day, there can be very different results.

Something that is becoming more and more scrutinized is the different styles employed by the top drivers.

Even drivers who are considered elite can possess a style that can mean success or failure on certain circuits in certain conditions and/or certain temperatures. This is how small the window to be competitive is nowadays and another reason why drivers who are attempting to make it need to be supremely accurate as they develop and deliver.

Sebastian Vettel has a distinctive style. When they get the car just right to suit that style, he absolutely flies and becomes untouchable. When they do not hit it right, we have seen that his teammate, Mark Webber, can go toe-to-toe with him. British journalist Mark Hughes says, "If there is a secret weapon to Sebastian Vettel's speed, it's his ability to live with rear instability on corner entry, enabling him to carry a lot of speed in. Like Lewis Hamilton he doesn't need to lean on one end or the other—he's relaxed about reacting to whatever it does. Others, such as Jenson Button, derive their speed by leaning very hard on the front of the car into the corner. They need a strong front and a predictable rear, and if the rear displays any instability it affects their confidence to carry the speed in. Vettel, like Lewis and Kimi Raikkonen, seems not to mind what the car will throw at him and just rides the wave. He'll use a spike of oversteer to hasten the direction change. He's not quite as audacious in this as Hamilton, but he can operate at a high level over the full range of handling traits, even if that's sometimes within the same corner."

This description clearly shows that the champions get their speed in different ways, but this final act fine tune I believe comes only after the fundamentals that are in this book are understood and developed. And if you intend to play in the Formula 1 paddock, they better be developed to the maximum, because many believe we are in the midst of the most competitive group of drivers ever in the history of the sport.

STAND-OUT CHAMPIONS

From all the drivers I have seen in the modern era, five stand out as being very special: four-time world champion Ayrton Senna from Brazil, four-time world champion Alain Prost, seven-time world champion Michael Schumacher and three-time world champion Sebastian Vettel. I make no apologies for choosing Formula 1 drivers, because I believe Formula 1 is the most competitive, intense and challenging form of motorsports on the planet. Very closely aligned with these four is double world champion Fernando Alonso. Alonso has that safe hands feel about him, whereas Vettel still has the young and inexperienced feel about him; he became world champion very quickly in a Red Bull car that was clearly superior to its rivals in 2010, 2011 and 2012.

These drivers were very different, but all became a part of history because of the way they applied themselves to the task of motor racing. Ayrton was emotionally driven, Michael is mentally driven, Alain was mission driven, as is Alonso and Vettel.

No matter what their physical and mental makeup is, there is no doubt if you want to emulate a great motorsports champion, you could not pick five better or different models than Senna, Prost, Schumacher, Alonso or Vettel. Throughout this book these five (particularly Schumacher and Vettel) will be contrasted with drivers of today and yesterday. It will be a fascinating uncovering of what makes the difference between a champion and a very good driver.

British journalist Mark Hughes offered this interesting insight between Senna, Prost and Schumacher:

"The impression is that the Ferrari [Schumacher's] cockpit is a rather colder, quieter place than was Senna's.

"However, to believe that all this order, rationality and cerebral control is more formidable than the hormonal rush of Senna at work is to discount the unbelievable territory to which those emotions—and probably his religious convictions too—gained Senna access. He could channel his feelings to pull out a qualifying lap like that at Monaco '88, where from within the deep reaches of his soul he found 2.5 seconds. Such things should not have been possible. At the same place the next year, he was playing nip and tuck with Prost for pole when, out of the blue, he produced a lap 1.0 second quicker than anything his rival could manage. Some even wondered if the timing machinery had malfunctioned.

"That is what Senna at his best could do—make you doubt your senses.

"Schumacher has many times produced performances that have reduced his opponents to bit players, but it has invariably been—like Barcelona '96—in compromised conditions. That day he was lapping sometimes six seconds faster than anyone else in the rain, and doing it with a lightness of touch that made it seem like child's play.

"Alain Prost was known as the Professor. He was meticulous in his preparation and his execution during a race was flawless. His pre-race planning was second to none and his emotional and mental control was admired at all times. Both Senna and Schumacher were known for emotional (and irrational) outbursts in the car, Prost never did such a thing. Senna was flamboyant, Schumacher was a machine and Prost was a calculator."

I believe however that the greatest example of a driver developing the complete package necessary to become a champion has to be Michael Schumacher (pre-retirement). He is the greatest driver of the modern era. Undoubtedly one of the greatest drivers of all time. Michael went through several crucial stages of his career, but he never lost sight of what his job ultimately was and what it would take to be the very best he could be. Michael had a fully developed Champion's Pyramid. As we have accurately seen of the past few seasons, the world of motorsports changes quickly. Of special interest is the return of Schumacher from retirement and then his subsequent second retirement. Were there elements of his package that changed as he made his return to Formula 1? I think his failure after his return was purely down to the fact that his skills at 40-plus years of age were just not as sharp as when he operated at his highest levels.

Perhaps the finest example of Schumacher's complete ability might be when he took an almost unprecedented step by moving to Ferrari from Benetton for the 1996 season. He was world champion with the Benetton team, and Ferrari at that time was not a good team. During his early and sometimes trying times, Michael drew upon his multiple on- and off-track skills as he set about building around him the type of environment he needed to win. He never criticized Ferrari, even when the car did not match his obvious skills. He always helped and supported the team, always had a smile even if he was not on the podium. He was building the crucial trust and belief within the team that was to be an almost unshakeable foundation.

Celebrated Irish journalist, and a good friend of mine, Maurice Hamilton also recognized Michael Schumacher's off-track abilities.

Maurice wrote in *America's Racer* magazine at the end of the 2002 season, "Since coming to the Modena in '96, he has been the catalyst most responsible for pulling racing's most celebrated team up from mediocrity to a period of unrivaled dominance. It was Schumacher, after all, who helped assemble the Ferrari brain trust of Jean Todt, Ross Brawn and Rory Byrne; and it's Schumacher who is adored and respected by the hundreds of anonymous engineers, technicians and mechanics who make the Scuderia fire on all 10 cylinders."

"A very big plus in his favor is the way he has worked very hard at molding that team around him," noted Maurice, "He took the hard route by choosing to go to Ferrari instead of Williams, has worked the team around him like nobody else has done, and has got this ability to work, work, work and have the total affection and the dedication of the team. That's always the sign of a good champion."

Even four-time world champion Alain Prost, affectionately known as The Professor, saw Schumacher as a special talent who understands how to create the right environment for him to flourish.

In a French magazine interview, Prost related how he admired the part Schumacher played in turning Ferrari around—that, and his ability to make a team revolve around him, much as Senna did: "That's the number one thing. Obviously, Michael took on a great challenge when he went there. The biggest challenge is to bring an unsuccessful team to the top, and, OK, Ferrari was not a small team, but it was not winning much. It was a difficult move from Benetton where he was world champion to Ferrari. He never criticized them even when the team and the car were not good; he always helped the team and he was always smiling when he was third or fourth. And I really like that about him. I think he has created a good ambience there and that's what I admire about him the most."

In 2002, British journalist Jonathan Noble talked with Michael and got a glimpse of why he is so great. "My philosophy is never to think you have achieved it," Michael said. "You always have to look at what you can do different and what you can do better with the car and with yourself. And you will always find little things. You have to do things differently because the moment will require it. You have to be flexible enough to see it and be open to see it."

Jonathan believed it is one of Schumacher's strengths that he consistently finds ways to boost his own motivation.

"But then the good thing is that you will do three days of going around and around and around with nothing happening, because you are working on the same area, and suddenly on the last day you find two tenths. Up goes your motivation again. You are always looking for it and you always feel that when something reasonable happens, it was worth it."

Noble also notes that Schumacher shone brightest in race conditions because of his innate ability in good, average and even bad cars. Ferrari sporting director Jean Todt said, "We know very well that Michael's biggest strength is to be able to get the best out of even a very difficult car to drive."

England's Mark Hughes has studied Schumacher from every angle. In a feature printed in England's premier motorsports magazine, *Autosport*, Mark had these fascinating insights into what I consider to be the most complete race car driver ever:

"Neither his driving style—early turn-in, not much steering lock, using the brakes to aid direction change—nor his racing style—flat-out attack start-to-finish, utilizing his supreme fitness to make every single lap count—have changed much over the years.

"It is the latter point that is remarkable. After more than a decade at the top of the sport, a driver will usually be relying less on raw speed, more on experience. That's how it was for Niki Lauda, say, or Alain Prost. But such an approach wouldn't be appropriate to today's [2002] fuel-stop format of Formula 1, where races comprise two or three stints of flat-out running and where looking after tires, gearboxes and engines isn't such an issue. Try to back off from the raw edge in this era, and you'd soon be discovered. There's no hint of it from Schuey.

"His lifetime fitness levels will have certainly aided him in keeping up his speed, as has his way of operating in a comfort zone. Having his own family of a team around him for virtually his whole career will surely have helped ensure his talent is less perishable to the years than it is for those drivers who operate in a war zone, fighting everyone and everything.

"There is no doubt Schumacher is joyous and charming if he wins, but he denies that his ruthlessness to defend his position in a race—most notably his fabled chops on rivals—is anything out of the ordinary.

"There is undoubtedly a degree of humbleness about Michael Schumacher. He clearly knows he is the best man out there at the moment, but steadfastly refuses to rub such a fact into his rivals."

"I pay as much respect to everyone—because we all eat, drink and come from the same base," Schumacher said.

Former Schumacher teammate at Ferrari, Eddie Irvine, said, "The easy bit is to be as quick as Michael in a good car. Far harder is to be anywhere near him in a bad one."

Then along came Sebastian Vettel who started obliterating Formula 1 records immediately upon his arrival. He was a phenom and he became one of the most scrutinized Formula 1 drivers ever. Why was he so good? What was so different? Was it just a superior car? Part of the answer is no, it was not just a superior car. He is exceptionally good, but we should not forget the support he has had from Red Bull from an early age. What many people don't know is that Vettel spent two days testing an Indy Car in Homestead, Florida, with Derrick Walker's team when he was 15 years old.

The two people who know and understand him best of all are his team manager, Christian Horner, and his technical director, Adrian Newey.

"Sebastian has tremendous natural speed and great intelligence within the car. He has the ability to think and adapt to many situations and is a driver with the rare combination of raw speed and the ability to make a vital contribution on a technical level. Like any human being, he makes mistakes, but he rarely makes the same mistake twice. He learns all the time," Adrian Newey says (Red Bull technical director in a discussion with Edd Straw).

"He has the ability to process things very quickly and he makes a very steep learning progression from his mistakes. His ability to withstand the pressure at the end of that year is what enabled him to become world champion. He is renowned as one of the hardest-working drivers, with a very clear idea of what he wants from the car," Newey adds.

The above was written before Vettel and Red Bull mounted their charge to his third world championship in 2012. Together they did what was needed. Now I know he had arguably the finest Formula 1 designer ever, Adrian Newey, by his side to provide him with the right car to do the job, but it's the driver's qualities you need to take note of and see if you can emulate some of these same elite athlete qualities. Newey believes the driver is central to a team understanding its car, no matter how much data is accumulated.

ENVIRONMENT MANAGEMENT

It is my belief that to extract the very best from any elite athlete you have to surround him with the type of environment that helps him flourish. That environment also has to be all-inclusive. In other words, it has to be an environment that allows a driver to be adequately equipped to then position himself for success. Plants grow well in the right environment, as do people.

The stars of Formula 1 and Indy Car flourish in the right environment. Junior drivers in their development years also need the right environment. When operating at the top of the tree, the right environment allows a driver to extract the maximum performance from himself. A junior driver needs the right environment to learn the right skills. Extracting the maximum performance cannot happen without having the right skills developed. When parents choose the right school for their children, they make the choice based on what the student might learn. When the children graduate, their diploma confirms they did in fact learn. Race teams are somewhat similar. They should be chosen during a driver's teen learning years based on what they will learn. A driver is born with the talent to drive. That never changes. What does change is the amount of knowledge and experience he adds to the talent package. With the right knowledge and experience added, this then allows him to extract the maximum performance from himself and his car. Adding the right knowledge and experience provides access to the performance the talent a driver is born with can deliver.

If you ever questioned why the right environment is important for drivers, consider what Renault Executive Director of Engineering Pat Symonds said to British journalist Mark Hughes in November 2004 about British Formula 1 Star Jenson Button. Jenson had a trying time at Renault, and, despite his talents, rewards were not forthcoming.

Button is regarded as having a driving style that is beautifully stylish—and very quick. His steering inputs are minimal and he appears to rely less on braking to aid direction changes, and the technical core of the team was unsympathetic to fine-tune the problems he was having in molding the car to his natural style.

Symonds now says, "I don't think we saw what we had. Everything we've seen subsequently suggests we failed to extract his potential."

At the Formula 1 world championship level (or any level), it's about finding your groove, locking onto it and molding things around you (environment) to hold that groove. Only then do you have full access to your talent, and that's rarely achieved.

When Frenchman Romain Grosjean was banned after yet another first lap crash at Spa 2012, his team manager Eric Bouillier took some of the blame for not creating the protective environment he deemed Grosjean needed. "It's not just mental. It's also my mistake in this case," said Bouillier. "I wanted Romain to be open because he was criticized in 2009 for being too arrogant and closed. Maybe I left the door open too long as everyone got used to Romain saying hello and people would always ask him questions. This disturbed his preparation, so I need to put the system in place, as with most drivers, where they have the proper environment."

Bouillier obviously believes a certain preparation routine that is somewhat protective of his rookie driver is the type of fine-tuned environment that would allow him to flourish without distractions.

It's that rarely achieved potential this book is designed to unlock. There is no magic to being successful in racing, but you do need to know how to find your groove, you need to know how to create the environment within which you will shine. You need to know how to position yourself for success. If you spend any time around me, you will hear me preach about the need to position a driver for success. I'll cover positioning in a later chapter.

You do need to know what to develop and how to develop it, and when you develop all areas of the Champion's Pyramid you will be a powerhouse, and, most importantly, you will be the best you can be. The right learning environment will accelerate your ability to learn and therefore perform at your highest level.

R-DNA

Every person on this planet is born with strengths and weaknesses. I don't believe a race car driver is ever born with all the strengths he needs to become a great champion. Every driver has a certain and unique makeup. I call it his Racing DNA or R-DNA. That R-DNA will be unique to him. It might be similar is some areas to other drivers, but, I assure you, it is unique to each driver. Within that R-DNA will be seven profiles on display every time a driver performs. These profiles are his strengths and weaknesses. These profiles are also his passport to success or failure. These profiles are also the window through which every driver is viewed.

Unlike your human DNA, your R-DNA can be altered. For example, everyone is born with a certain body shape; however, each one of us can determine how our bodies look and act. We can overeat and become less active or we can work at having a different and more active look and ability. What you look like is a product of decisions you make, and what you race like is a product of the decisions you make.

The first edition of *Race to Win* drew much praise for the communication chapter that specifically dealt with the four different personality temperaments. I had drivers call me saying that after reading it, they communicated differently with their children. A driver's temperament can have a great influence on how and what he learns. Temperaments are a big part of a driver's R-DNA.

Each person is born with the ability to choose and those choices determine how they think, look and behave. It's the capacity to choose that separates humans from any other creature on the planet. The right choices are fueled by your desire to be the best you can be or not. Remember: Choice equals change. Change can be threatening for many people because oftentimes it requires an element of discomfort and because it does expose your fears: fears of the unknown, fears of failure, or just fear of exposing your weakness.

How you perform as a driver is also a direct result of decisions you make. The level a driver achieves will be directionally proportional to the development of all areas of the Champion's Pyramid.

Throughout this book I will break down each of these profiles and show you through example what separates the good from the great.

WHAT IS DRIVER DEVELOPMENT?

It really is amazing to me that with so much at stake in big-time motorsports that there are so few structured driver development programs in America or Europe, especially compared to stick and ball sports. Even though motor racing is a complex and dangerous sport, it has usually relied on drivers self developing. Perhaps being so dangerous and complex is part of the reason it has become somewhat insular.

Driver assistance programs provide support, sometimes financial or sometimes just equipment. However, no matter what sponsorship or equipment you have, without all the skills necessary to get the best from it, it can be a wasted investment.

Why do you think other professional sports have team coaching and also specialized coaching for specific positions? How good would superstar NFL quarterback Peyton Manning or tennis star Rafael Nadal have become if they were subjected to generalized self-developed coaching, instead of specialized coaching? How good would Tiger Woods have become if he did not enjoy the benefits of specialized coaching? Just think how preposterous it would be to have no specialized coaching for soccer, NFL football, tennis or golf. Well, that's the situation motorsports largely finds itself in today. Everyone is left to fend for themselves.

Every sport in the world relies on specialized coaching, and motor racing should be the same. What if your son or daughter had access to the knowledge and had a chance to develop to become the next Michael Schumacher or Lewis Hamilton or even the next best thing? It could pay back huge dividends. Ferrari could never afford to buy the type of positive exposure Schumacher generated for them through his technical ability, his ability to energize the team and, of course, his sheer driving ability while winning five world championships. Is the $25 million (rumored) Ferrari paid him in his heyday expensive or good value? I think it is good value, because it's less than 10 percent of their overall race budget. McLaren backed Lewis Hamilton from the time he was 12 years old and he repaid them with stunning race wins and a world championship. Despite this, the sport in general does not invest in itself, especially in the U.S. Unlike all successful businesses where they reap what they sow, motorsports until about 2010 largely refused to invest, and therefore the development of champions and/or heroes was left somewhat to chance.

For many years certainly in the U.S., a variety of racing schools have promoted their driver development program. The reality is that most racing schools don't have the depth of knowledge or experience to truly know what it takes to develop a champion driver. Consider racing schools to be elementary schools and future champions need university curriculum.

Drivers need to be developed individually. Not only do they need to be accurately evaluated and then taught individually, but also they need to be made aware of what will be necessary when the big time comes knocking. Simply supplying money and equipment is like sending a student with a desire to be a scientist to a neighborhood school. Sure he will learn a lot and he will progress. But he will never reach great heights without specialized college tuition. Grids today are full of drivers who have been hugely successful relying on their instinct and reflexes. This book is designed to take you much deeper and give you a foundation that will not be easily rocked, and a knowledge that can make you the best you can ever be. No one can ask for more than that.

The key to real driver development is how you position yourself to get the very best from yourself and therefore reap the rewards and the financial benefits. No driver could ever complain if, during his career, he was able to become the very best he could be. To become the very best you can be in motorsports is not a black art. To develop a driver to be the best he can be is not a black art either. It is a clear path that must be understood and one that has always challenged drivers and particularly parents. One of the significant challenges is to understand what positioning for success is. Positioning is big in my book, because of the following context.

Think about a driver who starts preparing at a high level before he gets to the race track. He studies data, video, his reference points at each corner, etc., has his helmets (wet and dry) ready with all accessories available, has his suit ready to go, has all paperwork (license, etc.) taken care of, has provided all media quotes needed and has all flights and accommodation organized. He is now fully equipped and positioned for success and ready to take the next step.

He then gets to the race track and does his track walk, perhaps sits in the car if anything has been changed, debriefs with his engineer to understand the plan for the first practice session and takes care of any other pre-race activities. He now continues to be equipped and positioned for success.

In the first practice session the driver must be as mistake-free as possible, deliver accurate information to his engineer regarding the car setup for both chassis and engine to make the car as fast as anyone else's. He now continues to be adequately equipped and still positioned for success.

Next up is qualifying. Now the driver's job is to position himself on the track for traffic-free laps that get the best from new tires. Make any adjustments needed to balance the car on new tires, and, of course, do mistake-free laps with his actual lap time as close as possible to his theoretical best lap time. If he accomplishes this, he is now at the front of the grid and is again positioned for success.

When the race unfolds, the driver needs to get a good start to put himself in a position to control the race and keep himself positioned for success. During the race if the driver is mistake-free, if the pit stops are mistake-free and if any pit stop strategy is well thought out and executed, the driver will continue to be positioned for success. If all of the above are aligned more often than the competition, the driver remains positioned for success in races and championships at a higher level and on a more regular basis than the competition.

Now, it's virtually impossible to have everything as aligned as one would like every weekend. However, the sustained winners align more of the pieces than the competition on a more regular basis with deliberate actions.

What derails this success alignment are circumstances out of a driver's control and/or a driver's weaknesses. Outside circumstances such as other drivers' mistakes and/ or accidents, you can do nothing about except react as best you can and salvage the best result possible. A driver's weaknesses are something you can do something about and you need to do something about. As I mentioned earlier, I have yet to come across a driver who was not born with strengths and weaknesses. A driver's strengths might be his ability to drive fast, or raise the necessary funding, or technically set up the car, or communicate at a high level, or be physically fit enough, or be mentally bomb-proof, or possess the desire and commitment needed. The real key to this list is that anything on it can also be a driver's weakness, and any of these can and probably will be a driver's in-built restrictor. The drivers and/or parents who recognize any weakness, and get it developed into a strength (perhaps by adding a specific component coach?) will be on their way to success alignment and will therefore position the driver for success at a higher level and on a more regular basis. Admitting a weakness requires the strength of honesty and transparency.

This second edition of *Race to Win* is designed to help you understand the right path and provide you with some of the answers to the same questions all drivers and parents have, and it is designed to be an ongoing foundation and learning tool for driver development unlike anything available in motorsports today.

YOUTH MOVEMENT

Sebastian Vettel was testing an Indy Car (technically it was a Champ Car) at 15 years of age. This should not become the model for all young drivers. More drivers fail by jumping too fast than by taking deliberate slower steps.

Something all parents need to be aware of is the dangers of the more recent youth movement. The charge has been led by Sebastian Vettel and his success, but pushing drivers through the development stages too fast is a very slippery slope. Vettel's success has accelerated the perception that younger is better when the facts still remain that teen-agers can only process information at the rate teen-agers can process information. All human beings mature at their own pace depending on the environment they have been subjected to. The mature person then becomes the mature athlete.

Consider that the faster you push your child through the development process has to be directly proportional to the size of the funding available. The less the funding, the slower you should go, because you can't afford any hiccups. Mistakes made can be masked somewhat by the ability to purchase a second chance if it does not work out well the first time.

I see too many drivers pushed too far too fast because the parents make an emotionally laden decision as opposed to an intellectual decision. Graham Rahal told me he thought he went through the development series too fast, and when he got to Newman Haas as a 19-year-old Indy Car driver, he was ill-prepared for the pressures of that level. It might be a good argument that, after his initial success, he has struggled to establish himself as a star of the future. Michael Andretti would also slow his son Marco's development down if he had a second shot at it, as he also believes he went through the development phases too fast.

In 1994 another American, Elton Julien, went from a club race level in America to being the hottest property around and was lined up to get a Formula 1 test with the French

Larousse team. The test fell apart, so did the momentum and so did his career. It is my belief he was pushed through the system too fast. No matter how much talent a driver has, he has to acquire knowledge and experience to sustain his growth and success. There is no real shortcut to gaining that invaluable knowledge and experience.

Sebastian Vettel made it because he was extremely talented and had an open checkbook. Can you imagine a 15-year-old testing an Indy Car at Homestead Speedway with Walker Racing and having a checkbook available to pay for you to have access to those types of cars at such a young age? The downfall of this type of rapid rise is that it breeds a perception you have to make it to the top at a young age, which of course is not entirely true.

EARLY LEARNING DAYS IN FORMULA 1

The same principles of extracting speed from a team, driver and car is pretty much the same as when I drove for the March Formula 1 team in 1981. March founder/designer and my personal engineer Robin Herd, regularly said, "There is absolutely no magic to being successful in motor-sports. You just need a competitive driver, competitive car and enough money in the budget."

The budget is a crucial part of the equation. It will also be an ever-changing number that needs to be big enough to provide and service the equipment and personnel, and managed well enough to last the full season. The commercial side of a team can be very fractured and complicated and really needs to be handled by trained professionals.

The car is an ever-changing technical package that needs to be constantly adjusted and developed to give the best compromise of chassis setup for tracks and conditions. The team is expected to shoulder most of this load by working with accurate information from a driver and computer data to create a competitive race car. There is an indefinite number of settings that make up the best compromise for race car handling, and usually the stronger the engineering department of the team, the more accurately they can be at finding the right setup.

In my opinion, the driver is by far the most complex part of the puzzle, and by far the most important. The driver is an ever-changing and maturing package that needs to be constantly developed and well managed. The driver is the human element that is born with an R-DNA that is manifested through his physical, mental and spiritual attributes, but, more importantly the driver is born with both strengths and weaknesses. My hope is that as you read this, you will be open and honest enough to see yourself in the examples, and then you will set a path for yourself, armed with the new knowledge of what it takes to become a champion.

RELATIONSHIPS BECOME SPONSORSHIPS

One of the first things you need to know and fully understand is that motor racing is very much a relationship business. The first impressions you create can be long lasting. Your traits, strengths and weaknesses will become apparent to all the people who matter. All the teams talk to each other. Your driving talents will be the subject of discussion with any team owner/manager prior to hiring you. An element of early relationships young drivers need to understand is those relationships will be their sponsorships in their early days.

Team owners you meet at a very young age could well be your boss two or three decades later. The media will get to know and scrutinize your abilities and sometimes your life. They will sometimes be accurate and sometimes unfair, but they will always be there to report to the world just what their impressions of you are as a person, as a driver and as a team player. Remember their impressions may differ from your opinion, but their impressions are what will paint the picture for the many thousands who you will come in contact with you throughout your career. The media people you meet on the way up will also more than likely be around for all facets of your career.

Your traits, personality, strengths and weaknesses are the truth about your personhood, and the only thing that does not change is the truth. As soon as a driver enters a paddock, his book is being written. Just like a racehorse has a formbook, so does a race car driver. Every element of your personality, behavior, speed, strengths and weaknesses will become known very quickly. You can't hide anything in this sport.

EARLY PERSONAL RELATIONSHIPS

In 1965, the first motor race I saw as a young boy (12 years old) in my hometown of Dublin, Ireland, featured an English driver named Mo Nunn. Thirteen years later, I made my Formula 1 debut driving the Ensign Grand Prix car for the same Mo Nunn. Thirty-seven years later I was still working with Mo as I gathered information for my television duties featuring his Champ Car and IRL race teams.

In 1969 when a young Brazilian hot-shoe named Emerson Fittipaldi moved to England to develop his racing career, he started by racing in a Merlyn Formula Ford. Midway through the season he was in the Lotus Formula 3 team, and by the end of the year he was the British Formula 3 Champion. His two teammates were Dave Walker, the Australian who would partner Emerson just three years later in his first world championship-winning season, and Morris Nunn, who two decades later would engineer the Brazilian's Indy Car to a CART Champ Car championship win and an Indy 500 win. Both Emerson and Mo Nunn are good friends of mine today and willing resources when I do television work.

At a street circuit in Dunboyne, Ireland, in 1965, I was introduced to an Irish race car driver named Sidney Taylor. Twelve years later I was on the pole for the Formula 3 support race for the Austrian Grand Prix when Sid Taylor walked up to my mentor, Derek McMahon, and promised that if I won the race he would give me a test in a Formula

1 car. I won the race and less than six months later Sid was true to his word as he put me in to a brand-new design of Formula 1 car, the Theodore, built by Australian Ron Tauranac at Ralt Racing Cars.

In 1968 Ireland's only permanent motor racing facility, Mondello Park, opened for its first race meeting. I boarded a bus in Dublin City for the 35-mile drive. Little did I know the track was an additional five miles from the end of the bus route. At the end of the day, and not relishing the long walk back to the bus stop, I hitched a lift from someone with a single-seater race car on an open trailer. It turned out to be businessman Frank Keane, who was to become Ireland's BMW importer, and also who helped sponsor me in the European Formula 2 Championship 10 years later.

MEMORABLE IRISH MEETING

While I struggled to race in Ireland in 1975, I became aware of a large (about 300 pounds of large) Irish businessman named Derek McMahon. Derek was affectionately known as Big D. He raced successfully at club level in Ireland and England and was a significant figurehead in Irish motorsports. Big D was well known for the amount of alcohol he could drink in a day and still be as fresh as a daisy the next day, even with limited sleep.

During a race meeting in Kirkistown (near Belfast, Northern Ireland), I heard Big D was holding court at the bar. With my heart in my mouth, I summoned enough strength to approach him and ask if he would be interested in financially helping a young Irish driver who wanted to go to England and attempt to race professionally. He paused for a few seconds, swallowed hard, wiped his nose and face, looked at me a little sideways and blurted out, "Listen here, young monkey, I need you like I need a f%#@&ng six-inch hole in me head."

With that response, I left with the proverbial tail between the legs. I left for England the next season and went on to win 23 Formula Ford races. At the end of the year I managed to win the biggest event of the season, the Formula Ford Festival. It was a great season, but there did not seem to be any clear road forward because I did not have the financial wherewithal to continue.

I was planning for my return home to Ireland when out of the blue I got a call from Big D. He asked me to meet him at the Dorchester Hotel in London where he was attending the BRDC (British Racing Drivers Club) end-of-season prize giving. I walked in feeling like a fish out of water. That night Big D said he remembered my conversation of a year ago (even as short as it was) and he had followed my progress since then. He said he was impressed by my desire and commitment and he would financially back me in the British Formula 3 championship.

That relationship changed the direction of my life. Together we won the British Formula 3 championship in our first year together. Big D became my mentor and sponsor and backed me all the way to Formula 1. Thirty-one years later, I still call Big D and enjoy conversations about what we did together.

While living in England in 1976, I met and became friends with Ian Phillips, the editor of England's premier motorsports magazine, *Autosport*. Ian had a desire to help young drivers try to make their way through the clutter of motorsports, and we had many discussions about what I should do and how I should try to do it. Because Ian was the editor of the most significant motorsports magazine in England, he was a good resource for me to learn about the people and places that might be able to help me develop my career as a professional race car driver. Many times I would not have the funds to spend on a hotel room for the night and I would sleep on Ian's couch in London, with his dog Enzo. Enzo was named after Enzo Ferrari, and was a beautiful golden Labrador. Unfortunately for me, he had total freedom in the house and his favorite place to sleep was also on the couch, as the hair balls confirmed. For me, though, it was a cheap place to get some sleep.

Twenty-seven years later, I wanted to do a television show about my track testing the Jordan Formula 1 car at Silverstone in England. Speed Channel in America had agreed to broadcast the show and I put a production crew together using contacts in America and England. The person who provided me with total access to the Jordan team and who signed off on the project was none other than Ian Phillips, who was at that time in charge of business development at Jordan Grand Prix.

In 1982 Keke Rosberg and I drove for the Williams Formula 1 Team. Keke became world champion that year, and 20 years later his son, Nico, won the Formula BMW championship in Germany, and then tested the Williams BMW. After winning the GP2 championship in 2005, Nico was signed to be a full-time Grand Prix driver for Williams. Don't think for a minute Keke's ongoing friendship/ relationship with Frank Williams did not pave the way for the initial test and then the contract to race.

In 1976, I moved from Ireland to England to race Formula Fords. One of the strongest cars I had to race against was the Royale. The Royale factory was forever developing new parts and ideas. The Royale designer in those days was a little-known South African designer called Rory Byrne, who I developed a friendship and a great respect for. More than 25 years later my friendship is just as strong, although Rory was a little busier designing the Ferraris that carried Michael Schumacher to five of his seven world championships.

During those heady days of Formula Ford in England, one of my friends and close competitors was John Bright (who drove one of the very special Rory Byrne–designed Royales). Thirty years later I had a discussion with John Bright in the paddock in Daytona about how to get my son Conor to England to help develop his young racing career.

When I moved to England in 1976, I was introduced to Alan Henry and Peter Windsor. They were regarded as two of the best journalists of their day and wrote many stories about me during my days in Formula 1. Thirty years later, I still work with both of them on American Formula 1 television broadcasts.

Whether it is Earnhardt, Gordon, Alonso, Raikkonen, Button, Andretti or Bourdais, you will find all drivers have similar stories about long-term relationships. However, you will find the great drivers have been able to develop substantial relationships that usually end up paving the way for them to take significant steps throughout their careers. As great a driver as Michael Schumacher was, he also needed a little help from his friends. In 1990, his relationship with Mercedes sports car team owner Peter Sauber was such that Sauber paid for his first Formula 1 drive with the Jordan team.

These are just a few examples highlighting the fact that motorsports is a small family that is relationship-driven. One of the first things I say to young drivers is to get out and meet and mix with the people you want to race with. Get to the races, roam the pit lanes and introduce yourself to the principals. I remember having to do that when I started out and I was really bad at it. Because I was basically shy, I had to force myself to do it, and some of those relationships endure today.

There is a good and bad side to the business being relationship-driven. The bad side is that if you burn bridges it will more than likely come back to haunt you. The flip side is that by building and enhancing friendships and relationships, it can lead to more career breaks than sponsorship. Burning bridges can also highlight a personality trait that some teams just would not want to deal with. Successful teams are the result of the collective strengths of people working together in harmony and growing together through the good and bad days.

SIMPLE IRISH BACKGROUND

I was one of the very fortunate people who got to live my dream. I came from a working-class family background in Dublin, Ireland, where our family financial support initially came from the salary of a meat salesman before the family progressed to owning a corner grocery store. I had a typical working-class background living in an average neighborhood where we played soccer and amused ourselves with some of the simpler things of life. I was always mechanically minded, became interested in motorsports at an early age and clearly remember having to call our local newspaper to find out the results of Formula 1 races, because they were not covered by television (or even newspapers) at that stage. No one in our neighborhood knew anything about motorsports, as it was a sport that was for other people.

In 1965 when I was 12, I saw my first race on the streets of a small village on the outskirts of Dublin called Dunboyne. My dad drove me the 35 miles from our house for Saturday's practice, but I had to ride my bicycle out on Sunday because my dad was not available. Dunboyne was a typical Irish village with the usual grocery store, Catholic church, graveyard, and five or six pubs. It featured narrow roads and its signature section was a humpback bridge that claimed the lives of two people that weekend. Because of those deaths, 1965 was to be the last year ever for street racing in Dunboyne.

As I sat on the grass bank with soggy sandwiches in my backpack, I was not to know then that that weekend changed the course of my life. The sights, the noise and smells captivated me so much that they set me on a path I would follow for the rest of my life. The main reason I went was to see the brother of one of my dad's customers in his grocery store, Sidney Taylor. Sid had a white Brabham BT 8 he sometimes shared with future Formula 1 world champion Denny Hulme. Sidney had come to Ireland from England with his race transporter and was staying with his sister in our neighborhood. When I came home from school, there was an extra sense of excitement because my dad had arranged for me to see the race car inside the transporter. I still remember climbing up into the driver's seat and looking back at the white Brabham with the green stripe and the Irish shamrock symbol on the bonnet.

My own competition career started in 1969 when I made my debut in what we called stock car arcing in Santry Stadium, Dublin, driving an old Ford Anglia E93A.

My parents' contribution to my career was encourage-
ment with an overload of moral and emotional support.
One Sunday morning while attending the stock car races
in Santry Stadium, I met Jack Murphy, who had raced the
Anglia previously, but had blown the engine. The car lay
on the side of the road with a replacement engine sitting in
the boot. I paid him $15 and my dad towed the car home
on the end of a rope.

I was 16 years old at the time and rode my Yamaha 50cc
motorcycle to school every day. To get the budget to race,
even at such a low entry level, I needed to work. While I
worked at the local gas station, my dad fitted the replacement engine and my racing career was about to start. Before
I appeared at the track, I had to give my new race car a new
look. I scoured the tool shed at home for whatever house
paint was left over and Thunderbird was created using the
basic color scheme of typical 1960s home.

The track was a small dirt oval that promoted contact
as a path to success. In Ireland you cannot hold a driving
license to drive a car on the road until you are 18. Therefore
my dad had to tow the Anglia on the end of a rope across
the city to the track where my life's learning curve began.
Having a trailer was not an option in those days, as the
money available was just enough to buy a few sandwiches
for race day.

My road-racing career began in 1974 at the wheel of a
used Lotus 61 Formula Ford, purchased from former Jordan

Grand Prix team owner Eddie Jordan. I was 21, which was considered still young enough back then. My first test day, where we towed the car to the circuit with a rope, resulted in a crash through the trees that practically bent the car in half. That night at home I could hardly walk because of the pain in my right leg, yet it was not something I would dare tell my mother.

To get the budget to race in Ireland that year, I had my dad sign for a loan at the local bank on the pretense of opening a used-car business. I didn't believe the bank manager needed to know the used car in question was a used race car. I figured I needed the money to have any sort of chance of success and if it didn't work out, I had a lifetime to pay it back.

I had progressed to having an open trailer at this stage, but the cars I towed were a little on the sketchy side. Road-racing success came fast for me, winning a variety of public road hill climbs, and I actually managed to win my fifth ever road race, in the wet, at our local track, Mondello Park. To supplement my income I was now working at a local car repair shop where I could also prepare the race car.

AUSTRALIAN IRON ORE LABORER

At the end of that season I had not repaid the bank loan and needed more money to upgrade my race equipment for 1975. The only options I knew of to make big money, fast, during the winter, was either to work in the oil fields of

Alaska or the iron ore mines of Australia. The Alaskan oil fields required special warm clothing that cost almost $1,000 and that expense would be taken from my pay packet every month until paid back. Australia required old T-shirts and shorts, so, five days after I found out about the opportunity, I was in the middle of Perth, Australia, committing to be a laborer in the iron ore mines of Northwest Australia.

It was an amazing odyssey. Myself and other dreamers were put on a small plane in Perth, which headed straight north. As we swooped in for landing, I was scouring the ocean waters to see if I could see sharks. When we exited the plane onto the dirt runway, we were greeted by 90-degree heat, blazing sunshine and flies—lots of flies. We were packed into the back of an open truck and driven across the dirt roads of the bush to what we soon would know to be single men's quarters. Until there was a room available in the town, we had to live in wooden buildings in rooms that were approximately 10 feet by 6 feet. This was to be my home for the next six months, and the next step to chasing the dream.

Cliffs Robe River mining town in Wickham, Northwest Australia, was the scene of the hottest, dirtiest and hardest thing I had ever done in my life. We mixed with the roughest class of humanity who thought nothing of settling an argument with a knife or a gun.

The key to making big money in the iron ore mines was the number of hours you could put in for a two-week period.

Every Friday payday (biweekly) fellow dreamers would gather in the food mess hall and look how many hours were booked. The first eight-hour shift paid the regular hourly rate, the second eight hours paid double-time, but if you could work 24 hours straight, the final eight hours would pay triple-time. That's what the aim was for many of the more determined.

There were people from all walks of life there with different reasons for needing cash. Some wanted to buy houses, some wanted to pay off debt, many were drug addicts who needed the feed their habit and one in particular, Richard Burgess, was there to finance the purchase of a yacht.

After six months of toil, sweat and fun digging iron ore, I returned to Ireland with $5,000. It was more money than I had ever had before. The dirt of the mines gave me the chance to purchase a used Crossle 25F Formula Ford race car from my best friend, Gary Gibson. The iron ore laborer was now ready to continue his racing career in 1975.

THE DREAM BECOMES REALITY

The 1975 season was a classic, with me winning most of the significant races in Ireland, setting most of the lap records and winning the Irish Formula Ford championship. However, it didn't go according to plan initially. My new (to me) race car was almost good enough to win. I was almost on the pace, but at Mondello Park I destroyed it in a big crash midway through the season, and at that stage I thought my career was effectively over. I had spent most of the Australian money, and as we surveyed the wreck on the open trailer, the owner of the Crossle car company, John Crossle, walked up to me and offered to take the wreck in exchange for a brand new state-of-the-art Crossle 30F. He had obviously regarded me a driver who might be able to win some races in his car and therefore other people might buy more cars. This was to be the first significant break of my career. Armed with the brand new car, I dominated the second half of the season and won just about everything, including the Irish championship.

LEAVE HOME FOR GOOD

For the 1976 season I got upgraded to racing internationally, in England. My personal wealth (which was mainly tied to the worth of my race car) enabled me to either race or live reasonably, but I could not do both at the same time. As racing was the priority, I bought an old school bus, removed the seats, cut the back out, built two wooden ramps and rolled my Formula Ford inside my mobile home and workshop. The toolbox sat on one side, the race car was in the middle and the sleeping bag was on the other side. I said goodbye to my family, goodbye to my homeland, and went on to win 23 races, including the most prestigious end-of-season Formula Ford event of the year, the Tribute to James Formula Ford Festival. The 1976 FF Festival was so called to honor England's reigning Formula 1 world champion, James Hunt. James presented me with the trophy and it was a very proud moment for me and my family, who were all in attendance.

In 1977 the rocket ship really started to take off. Armed with financial backing from Irish businessman Derek McMahon, better known as Big D, and a Chevron B38 Toyota Formula 3 car, I started to pursue the British Formula 3 championship. The British Formula 3 championship was always, and indeed still is, regarded as by far the most prestigious F3 championship in the world. Pretty much any driver who won that championship, or who showed really well, went to Formula 1. Drivers who have followed this path include Ayrton Senna, Nelson Piquet, Eddie Irvine, Derek Warwick, Johnny Herbert, Jenson Button, David Coulthard and Jonathan Palmer.

That season was one of extremes, tears and joy all within the space of a few races. It was a time before the large transporters, team managers and engineers. We basically ran with one mechanic who was the team manager, chief mechanic, gofer and engineer all rolled into one. We converted a small van and ran the car inside on some wooden planks mounted on concrete blocks. We towed a small (trailer) caravan behind. We had just one car, one spare engine and no spare parts.

Midway through the season it all began to come together. Although I had yet to win a race, at the British Grand Prix support race I lead for many laps before crashing out with my archrival, Stephen South. I practically cried after the race when I tried to explain what happened to Big D. Two weeks later at the Austrian Grand Prix Formula 1 race, the support event again was for Formula 3 cars. The circuit was the famous Osterreichring, which was the fastest circuit I had ever been on. I was on the pole with future three-time Formula 1 world champion Nelson Piquet beside me on the front row. We were both combatants in the British championship, but this was the most prestigious event either of us had ever competed in.

Just before the start, Irishman Sid Taylor (the same Sid Taylor who I had gone to see race in Ireland in 1965), who handled Hong Kong businessman Teddy Yip's Formula 1 involvement, walked up to my mentor Big D and told him that if I won the race he would give me a Formula 1 test at the end of the season.

After a classic Formula 3 battle between Piquet and myself, I won the race that day and went on to win the last five races in a row back in England, and won the British championship. It was a fairy-tale ending you thought would only happen to other people—and it was happening to me.

The run of success at the end of that season in England started at Brands Hatch, and as I came down the stairs from the victory podium, I met a surprise visitor. Richard Burgess, who I had shared many a night shift with in the iron ore mines of Australia, was there to greet and congratulate me.

Richard had arrived in England on board the yacht he had bought from the proceeds of his days as a laborer in the iron ore mines of Australia. What joy we had that season.

Toward the end of the season I had a call from Guy Edwards enquiring if I would be interested in driving his ICI-sponsored Chevron Formula 2 car at Estoril, Portugal. in the penultimate round of the European Formula 2 championship. Big D again stepped up with some sponsorship funding and I was ready to take the next step up the ladder.

I had never seen the car before, never saw the track until the first lap I did in practice, and after the first qualifying session McLaren Chairman Ron Dennis (he owned a Formula 2 team at the time called Project Four) walked into our pit in disbelief at my lap time and said, "If Daly did that lap time, I'll eat my hat."

In the next session I went even faster and blew off his drivers, Italian-American Eddie Cheever and Brazilian Ingo Hoffmann. I had a spectacular weekend, finishing in fifth place and having set a new lap record that stood for six years until Grand Prix returned to the track in 1984. Guy Edwards, who was an ex-Formula 1 driver and who now concentrated on acquiring sponsorship of the team, was sufficiently impressed to become my manager.

FORMULA FORD TO FORMULA 1 IN 13 MONTHS

In December 1977, just as he had promised, Sid Taylor gave me a test in a brand-new Theodore Formula 1 car at

Goodwood, one of the most famous old circuits in England. The car had just been designed and built by Australian designer and owner of Ralt Racing Cars, Ron Tauranac. The F1 project had been financed by Hong Kong businessman Teddy Yip, who I would drive for the following year, as he was one of the principal backers of Mo Nunn's Team Ensign.

After my first run I realized I had gone from Formula Ford to Formula 1 in 13 short months. The fastest I was aware of at that time was Emerson Fittipaldi, who accomplished the feat in 18 months. It was an awesome accomplishment I probably did not fully appreciate at the time it was happening, because I was in the middle of my typical young, hungry invincible driver stage and was mostly unaware of anything outside of my immediate environment.

Having easily sailed through the lower formulae, when I got to Formula 1 it seemed the same vital momentum every career needs began to desert me. I began to struggle and things just did not keep going my way in Formula 1 as they had before. It all seemed so much more difficult and I began to try harder and harder and began to make mistakes at crucial times.

I was driven by the stopwatch and not by how the car felt. I drove for some great teams such as Tyrrell and Williams, but squandered the opportunities. I was just out of synch, and instead of controlling my own destiny with proactive decisions, I was becoming reactive to my environment. I did not seem to have a strong enough foundation to fall back on and the struggle went on for five years.

My big break came in Formula 1 when I joined the great Williams Grand Prix team in 1982. They did not have the fastest car that year, but they had the most reliable car and one that was fast enough to make a difference. I married my childhood sweetheart, Siobhan Ryan, at the end of 1980, and even that relationship became a burden to me because I was not equipped to handle it. I had flashes of brilliance all through the 1982 season, but I never connected the dots and never drove with the flair and ease I had in the lower formulae.

Probably the defining moment of the season came when I was leading the Grand Prix of Monaco. While rounding the Rascasse hairpin to start the last lap, my Williams stopped without any drive. The drive was lost because I had wiped the rear wing off in a half spin at Tabac corner while I was charging toward the front of the field. It was another error that proved very costly. For the rest of the season, I could never put any consistent performances together and made too many mistakes. At the end of the year, Frank Williams fired me, and after two years of marriage I went through a divorce, which finally derailed me. Although I didn't know it at the time, my weak mental skills became my restriction.

AMERICA, THE LAND OF CURIOSITY

At the end of the 1982 Formula 1 season, my boss Frank Williams phoned to let me know Jacques Lafitte would be replacing me in the Williams FW08C for the upcoming season. I didn't blame him one bit, as I knew full well I had not performed well enough to keep my seat. Soon after that I left for America to start the next phase of my career amongst the high-speed ovals of American Indy Car racing.

My first race was organized by a journalist friend of mine, Jeff Hutchinson, and an agent, Ted Quackenbush. I arrived in Phoenix, Arizona, in October 1982, to see the car and meet the team. Coming from the world of Formula 1, I was quite shocked with what I found. The team was owned by enthusiasts Herb and Rose Wysard, who ran a 200-mph race car at a standard lower than I had run Formula Ford cars in Ireland. It looked so shabby I joked with Ted I needed a tetanus injection to sit in the thing. The first time I pressed the throttle pedal it stayed on the floor. Apparently the previous driver, John Paul Junior, had gone off the road and punched the floor up into the throttle pedal assembly, and that now jammed the pedal. No one had thought to fix it. After much soul searching, I decided to try to race it, to at least get a feel for what oval-track racing was all about. I qualified ninth, beside American Johnny Rutherford, but the engine blew up halfway around the first lap.

I made my Indianapolis 500 debut in 1983. In September 1984, I was almost killed in a devastating crash at the Michigan International Speedway. I somehow survived the hardest impact that anyone had survived up to that time (approximately 210 mph).

It was September in Michigan and we were running the second Indy Car race of the season at Michigan International Speedway, the 200-miler. I was driving for Tony Bettenhausen's Provimi Veal–sponsored team and we were struggling a little to find the speed of the front-runners. I remember my first laps, and they were jaw-dropping to say the least. The first time I went flat-out into turn one, the G forces created by the high banks were so high that my helmet was literally pushed down on my head so much that it partially covered my eyes. It was borderline scary hard to believe a car traveling that fast could somehow go around a 180-degree corner.

About 20 laps into the race, I was lapping at 219 mph, which was faster than I had qualified. The track had a bump going into turn three and every time the car would go over the bump it would bounce up slightly, then settle down with an increased grip level on the right rear and the car would take a set and power through the corner flat-out from there. It was a rhythm repeated every lap. Lap after lap the same feel from the car would be transmitted to me and I felt as if I was just on the edge of adhesion.

On lap 26 it all went wrong. A slight mist began to fall and the grip level was slightly reduced as the car landed on the other side of the bump. Whereas the car usually landed with an increased grip level on the right rear tire, this time the tire gave up and the car began to spin.

It spun so fast that it threw my head back against the headrest. When I realized I was in big trouble, I clearly remember saying to myself, "Oh, shit!" and I remember pulling my legs back as far back as I could into the cockpit.

I have no memory of what happened in the next 15 seconds or so. Even when I look at the photos, it's hard to connect personally with the destruction. The car hit with such blunt force that it literally exploded and disintegrated into multiple separate parts. The front of the car, including the dashboard bulkhead and half of the cockpit literally broke off. I was left strapped to the back half of the tub without any frontal protection, and with my body exposed to a second and potentially fatal impact against the outside wall.

John Paul Junior (the same John Paul Junior who had driven the Wysard car before in 1982) decided that for him to miss the crash he would go high on the banking in attempt to drive around the carnage. His decision saved my life, because as he arrived on the scene I was mere feet from the wall and still doing over 100 mph. He hit me broadside, lifted my car clear off the ground and spun me down toward the infield. Within minutes the mist had turned to rain and the race was canceled for the day.

About two seconds before the wreck stopped rolling down off the banking, I was alert again. I was dazed but felt no pain. I began to do the physical check of legs, torso, right arm/hand, but when I got to the left arm I felt a chilling fear because I could not feel it. I immediately thought that I had suffered the same fate as my team manager, Merle Bettenhausen, who had suffered a similar accident in Michigan and he had his left arm severed. I used my right hand to grab through the facemask of my helmet and pull my head down enough to see that my left arm and hand, although bloodied, in fact was still attached.

The head of CART's safety team, Dr. Steve Olvey, arrived and knelt down in front of me and directed the team as he stared into my eyes. Steve Edwards then leaned over and talked to me. Just as Steve got up to attend to the cleanup, I reached up and grabbed him by his collar and in a scared, broken voice, pleaded with him not to leave me. It was only then that I realized just how scared I was.

I suffered severe injuries to my left ankle, left leg, hip, ribs, pelvis, and also had a toe amputated in the accident. I had a lacerated liver, mild head injuries, and very painful third-degree burns on my left arm. I was in intensive care for a week in the University of Michigan hospital before being transported via Lifeline to Methodist Hospital in Indianapolis. I required a total of 14 surgeries, including bone and skin grafting over the following two years, and then about four years of physical therapy followed. The accident certainly rocked my world and changed my views on many things.

I was sure I wanted to go back to racing again, and every day was dedicated to becoming physically and mentally as strong as possible so as I could take full advantage of whatever opportunity might come along.

During my recovery period, I began to get more and more interested in television broadcasting. In 1985, I signed a contract with America's best-known sports cable channel, ESPN. That contract was to last for the next 10 years, with me covering everything from Formula Ford to Formula 1. In addition to my racing career, I began to travel the world for television duties also.

I also spent a great deal of my time studying drivers, and pondering why some of them, with what seemed to be similar driving talent, seemed to achieve more success than others. There seemed to be some traits the champions possessed, and I began to study what they were.

I went back to racing on a full-time basis in mid-1987, but I knew that after my injuries I was never as good a driver again. I realized I could not mentally bring myself to my pre-accident state. This mental aspect prompted me to delve a little deeper into what else would be needed to bring me personally to a higher level as a driver. I raced until 1992 and won the biggest international races of my career, the 1990 and 1991 Sebring 12-Hour race, before I retired in 1992. Little did I know I would learn more about what I needed to compete after I retired from active competition.

REALITY CHECK

The reality of it was that my near-fatal accident put me on a learning path I hope can positively influence many others in the years to come. It was only years after I retired from competition I realized drivers have strengths and, more importantly, weaknesses. I had not recognized my own personal weaknesses and therefore I had not worked at turning those weaknesses into strengths. I believe those personal experiences are a valuable asset I can now pass on to the next generation of race drivers, and I will get just as much satisfaction from seeing them succeed.

Throughout my career as a race car driver, I was always deeply involved in what I was doing at that particular time, and I did not focus very much on what made the difference between winning and losing.

Naturally, I was so focused that I believed my strengths alone were enough to carry me through and I ignored my weaknesses. In fact, I never recognized or admitted I had any weaknesses. Perhaps I was too arrogant, or just afraid if any weakness was ever exposed it might somehow stall my progress. The reality is every team manager knew my weaknesses, and I now know that exposing my weaknesses early in my career would have made me a much more effective driver and could have changed the way my career developed. This is a large part of what I want young drivers to realize with the help of this book.

For many years, while I competed in Formula 1, Indy Cars and World Sports Cars, I had ample opportunities to both race against and mix socially with some of the best drivers in the world. I was part of a great era with drivers such as Mario and Michael Andretti, Ronnie Peterson, Rick Mears, Bobby Rahal, Niki Lauda, Alain Prost, Al Unser, Gilles Villeneuve, Nelson Piquet, Nigel Mansell, Emerson Fittipaldi, Johnny Rutherford and Jody Scheckter.

While in the television booth, I then observed closely great champions such as Michael Schumacher, Ayrton Senna, Michael and Mario Andretti, Nelson Piquet, Gil de Ferran, Alex Zanardi, Juan Montoya, Kimi Raikkonen, Tony Stewart, Jeff Gordon, Dale Earnhardt and Fernando Alonso, etc. Although they all have different strengths and weaknesses, they have all consistently shown they have the abilities not only to drive a car fast, but also to create and then manage their respective environments that can potentially put them in a position to be consistently successful. Note that I say *potentially,* because as you go through this book you will realize that some of them almost get to the top and some of them might never get there.

So what is it that separates the consistent winners from the pretenders? What is it that makes some drivers special? Why do some drivers become champions and others never seem to reach their potential? This book gives you the answer to that question. The answer has the potential to send you on the road to stardom by detailing clearly what you need to develop the skills to give you the ability to become a true champion.

Throughout this book I will give examples of current and past star drivers in an effort to clearly show the differences between drivers who have all the key elements and drivers who do not. As often as I can, I will use real-life scenarios in an effort to paint a clear picture of the often subtle differences between having the skills and almost having them. I will use documentation from respected journalists who follow every step of these drivers, and you will probably see yourself in some of the examples. Remember, it is becoming more and more difficult to make it to the top in racing because there are so many drivers these days who have access to a great deal of the required information. In addition, and largely because Formula 1 is so big, there are countries willing to back their athletes. The global platform an athlete has when he waves a country's flag is so enormous (Formula 1 is the largest-watched sport in the world) that a great deal of competition for seats at the very top is now flush with money. In Pastor Maldonado's case, he apparently took as much as $15 million to Williams and they therefore ousted Rubens Barrichello.

Think of what happened to Nico Hulkenberg in 2010. Just after scoring a scorching pole position in the wet at the Brazilian Grand Prix, he was fired to make way for a pay driver. People were aghast, but this is the reality of today's racing environment. This is further proof you cannot leave anything to chance. If you are fully developed, you may get your chance. If you are not fully developed, the odds stack up against you at a faster rate than any other sport I know.

I hate to say this, but I believe a very good driver with sponsorship money (there are many) will stand a better chance of getting the seat before true world-class talent might. If by sheer chance you do make it to the top without all the elements fully developed, I promise you, you will not have the staying power you might have. Motor racing at the highest levels is an unforgiving sport, and it is impossible to hide a weakness for very long. With all the ingredients fully developed, you will at least stand a chance of making it and have an opportunity to sustain your position at the top for a longer period.

Becoming a champion is not a game of chance, but it can be a game of choice. You may read several times in this book that choice is one of the most powerful words in the English language. The greatest power we all possess is the power to choose: choose whether we want to dedicate ourselves to becoming the very best we can be, choose whether you are prepared to put in the big effort, choose whether you are prepared to be completely honest with yourself and expose your weaknesses and then work on them, choose whether you are a listener and then an activator, choose where you set your target and move heaven and earth when necessary to hit it.

If you develop the Champion's Pyramid as much as you possibly can, you might not become a world champion, but you will definitely become the very best you can be. What more can you ask for?

TWO

TALENT IDENTIFICATION

*Were you born with a predominately
instinct-reflex talent, is it a feel-sensitive talent
or is it a combination of both?*

*Talent Identification

AFTER YEARS OF SEMINARS resulting from the interest in the original *Race to Win*, this chapter drew more comment from drivers and families when they fully understood its power. This is the Derek Daly Academy's holy grail. This is our anchor in the ground as DDA pioneered the understanding drivers could have different types of talent. Most people had never considered there could be two types of talent a driver can be born with. Neither one or the other is right or wrong, but they each need different types of support during the development stages. Again I will reiterate, talent identification is the very foundation of accurate driver development, because it provides the path and direction to ensure you are providing your driver with the right type of support. Make sure you are doing the right things as opposed to doing things right.

In 1997–1998, when CART team owner Barry Green from Team Green asked us at Derek Daly Performance Driving Academy in Las Vegas to create an American driver development program on behalf of tobacco giant Brown & Williamson, we had the opportunity to work with 46 of the most talented young drivers in the U.S. over a three-year period.

Racing drivers' styles are just like their personalities and looks, completely different in almost every way. It was a fascinating exercise that quickly exposed both the strengths and weaknesses of each driver. Each driver had to come by himself without any moral support from family or friends. Within hours, each driver's profile started to emerge, and with the types of exercises they were challenged with, they could not hide anything from us.

As the program progressed, some drivers were intimidated, some used the "book of excuses," yet some welcomed the opportunity and relished the competition. Some drivers went fast immediately and some took their time to get comfortable. Some drivers coped with adversity well and some got flustered. To do the same lap times, some got there aggressively using more tires, brakes and fuel, while some got the lap times with ease and finesse. It was fascinating to see the different styles and approaches unfold in front of us.

After three days' initial evaluation, we pretty much knew the strengths and weaknesses of the drivers with real potential. We also realized for each of the drivers to progress up the ladder to stardom, they would need individually tailored programs to suit their particular profile, just like a football player, skier, swimmer or any elite world-class athlete.

Racing drivers by their very nature are an ego-driven group who are almost scared to think someone would know that they have a weakness. This is their first big mistake that could derail a career. Truth and honesty in the early stages can create an unshakable foundation for a young driver. Just like the stopwatch never lies, the truth is the only thing that never changes.

The most important thing to remember is just about every young driver I have worked with has a profile of strengths and weaknesses. Recognizing and developing the weaknesses is the key to building what we now know as the Champion's Pyramid. If we take it that every driver has God-given talent, one might assume the strengths and weaknesses could be technical, communication (people skills), emotional or mental areas. However, as we delve into what type of God-given talent a driver might have, you begin to expose the foundation that must be clearly understood first.

I believe all potential great racing drivers are born with an inherent ability to understand the dynamics of a vehicle at high speed. They have an ability to feel through their backside what a car will do before it does it, which is vital at a place such as Indianapolis. They have a message delivery system from the butt cheeks to the brain that is permanently connected. They just *know* that when a car slides, you steer into the slide to regain control. You can't teach this instinctive reaction. It's just like when something is about to hit you. Your natural instinct causes you to put your hands up to protect yourself. This is instinctive, nobody taught you this.

The next question: What type of driving talent were you born with? Is it predominantly *instinct-reflex* talent, is it *feel-sensitive* talent or is it a combination of both. *Instinct-reflex* talent is a driver who can drive the wheels off anything he gets into. Whatever speed the car can go, he will make it go that speed. This would be a Lewis Hamilton, Tony Kanaan,

Juan Montoya, A.J. Allmendinger or a Kimi Raikkonen. These drivers are not known for strong technical feedback. These are gifted drivers who are well liked in a team because you know every time they get in the car, the speed they extract is all the speed the car has. The down side is that the team must know how to set up the car to get its maximum speed. The driver is too busy driving hard and fast to feel what the car is doing, and therefore the driver does not lead the team technically.

The *feel-sensitive* type of talent is a driver who can feel what the car does and can engineer the car to go faster. This would be an Al Unser, Bobby Unser, Gil de Ferran, Alex Zanardi or Jeff Gordon. These drivers can take bad cars and accurately identify the right changes necessary to engineer the car to go faster.

INSTINCT-REFLEX DRIVER

So let's delve deeper into the driver. These *instinct-reflex* drivers have nerve endings that are on fire and every fiber of their bodies are fully charged and ready to be unleashed as soon as they put a helmet on. Early in their careers an *instinct-reflex* driver becomes popular because he is usually a no-nonsense driver who just gets the job done. He is uncluttered with few distractions and only thinks about going fast. Engineering the car to go faster is not a high priority for him, because that is not in his character, and often they feel invincible. In the lower formulae they can get away with this because there is not a very complicated setup needed to be fast. Races tend to be short, tires tend to be spec, and therefore a flat-out sprint type of driver can be desirable. As long as a team can provide him with a good setup, he will happily do the rest.

Mika Hakkinen was fortunate to be a McLaren driver in a high-tech era where engineers and computers could provide him with the setup for him to use his *instinct-reflex* style. Because the late '70s or early '80s required a lot more accurate technical feedback from the driver, I don't believe Hakkinen would have been as successful then.

Many think one of Jean Alesi's biggest mistakes in his career was moving to Ferrari when he could have gone to Williams. Ferrari lured him through the emotional appeal, but they did not provide him with the cars good enough to take advantage of his phenomenal *instinct-reflex* style. Some think Williams could have provided him with a better car at that time in his career. What Alesi needed to become a champion at that time was a team that could provide him with a good car with minimal technical setup input from the driver. In this type of environment, I believe Alesi would have been more successful.

The *instinct-reflex* driver can also frustrate a team, because no matter how hard he drives, he might be just a little off the pace because he never thinks hard enough about the car setup and relies too much on other people to control his destiny, and, again in the lower formulae, it is easier to get away with it. Many go-kart drivers are *instinct-reflex* drivers because they are surrounded by tuners who set up their karts for them. This act, although well meaning by parents who write the checks to pay the tuners, can very often sabotage the future and long-term development of the driver because they fail to develop the discipline of making themselves think about what the car (or kart) is doing when they are in their formative learning years.

FEEL-SENSITIVE DRIVER

The drivers who are born with the *feel-sensitive* natural talent can travel a similar path in their formative years, but tend to have a bit more control of their destiny because they have the ability to guide the team technically. For the *feel-sensitive* driver it's always a fine line between trying to get the perfect setup and just going out and doing it. The technical driver has to walk the fine line between knowing what he needs in the car, but being fully prepared to give his all even if the car is not perfect. The *feel-sensitive* driver could also frustrate a team because he might not give his all if the car does not feel just right. Dario Franchitti and Jenson Button have a reputation for being like this. However, when the car is right, look out, because then they are a quick as anyone.

For the overall success of a team, it is vital for a driver and team owner/manager to understand exactly what type of talent he has and what part of the team needs to be supplemented to get the best from the driver. The real magic for a team manager is to understand this principle and have one of each in the team. The *feel-sensitive* driver is relied upon to find the best setup for the car and the *instinct-reflex* driver drives the wheels off it. This in turn pushes the *feel-sensitive* driver to push himself to his personal limits. Two top-line drivers pushing themselves and the car to the limits of possibility is usually a recipe for success within a team.

The team has to be properly set up, however, to take full advantage of such conditions. For example, one lead engineer might be enough for Indy 500 winner Gil de Ferran, or two-time world champion Fernando Alonso or four-time Champ Car champion Sebastien Bourdais because they are good at sorting out the right technical setup of the race car. Two-time Formula 1 world champion Mika Hakkinen or Grand Prix winner Jean Alesi and certainly Juan Montoya might need two or three engineers to make up for their lack of ability to provide accurate technical feedback.

A great example of a team who had the right combination of drivers at one time was Andretti-Green Indy Car team with Dario Franchitti, Bryan Herta, Tony Kanaan and Dan Wheldon. Dario and Bryan were the two *feel-sensitive* drivers while Tony and Dan were the *instinct-reflex* drivers. With this combination, the team was dominant.

Dario left for the Ganassi team and then Bryan retired to be replaced by Danica Patrick and Hideki Mutoh. With this combination of drivers, it's a good argument to say the vital *feel-sensitive* driver was gone and therefore the setup information was not as strong, and over time the team lost its way technically.

THE MAGICAL COMBINATION AND POWER OF BOTH

This is where the great complete champions come from. The champions are those who have sustainable power. The champions who have long careers at the very top of their profession. This list of drivers tends to be a little shorter. At the top of this list is Michael Schumacher. The unwashed might say Michael won so many races because he had the best car. That is absolutely right, but how do you think he got the best car? Because he is one of the most technically accurate drivers ever in Formula 1 and the most ruthless and focused driver on the track.

All through his lengthy career (except maybe after his return from retirement), no matter what the technical regulations were changed to, Michael could consistently lead a team in the right direction while developing the car. Poor technical feedback always resulted in longer car development times for some race teams.

Former Formula 1 world champion Damon Hill also had good technical feedback, and he ended up with a championship-winning Williams at his disposal. I believe his Formula 1 career ended abruptly because Frank Williams did not fully understand his contribution on the technical side, and he believed a potentially faster driver would be more beneficial to the team. When Damon Hill left, so did a strong influence in the technical direction of the team. History shows Williams did not have a really fast car until 2012 when the accurate input of Rubens Barrichello paid dividends.

Drivers can develop the magical combination of both *feel-sensitive* and *instinct-reflex*. This is when you have the ability to engineer a car to go faster, but when the chips are down, and the conditions are perhaps not favorable with the car just not to your liking, you are still able to drive it as fast as it can go despite the problems. This might be a Michael Schumacher, Fernando Alonso, Sebastian Vettel, Will Power, Mario and Michael Andretti, Alain Prost, Jackie Stewart, Sebastien Bourdais and Jimmie Johnson. Notice that these names are all multiple champions.

DISCIPLINE OR LACK THEREOF

Now let's deal with the driver who has other tendencies. What about the driver who has good technical feel in the race car, but does not have the discipline to concentrate on the setup work because all he wants to do is go fast? I know this type of driver very well, because I was like this. I didn't know it at the time, but, on reflection, it is now very obvious to me.

At the British Grand Prix, on the weekend of my Formula 1 debut, my team owner and engineer was Mo Nunn, of Zanardi, Fittipaldi, Andretti and Montoya fame (he was their engineer). I drove the Ensign MN01, which was a very efficient F1 car that gave good feedback. After Friday's qualifying, I was in the top 15, and because of this Goodyear rewarded us by allowing us to have a new-construction front tire for the final qualifying on Saturday. This would obviously help us stiffen up the front of the car and hence give us better traction. During the final one-hour session, with me trying to qualify for a Grand Prix for the first time, I did my first run on the control tires in preparation for the new tires made with latest and greatest construction. My first run put me 12th on the grid and a ripple of excitement ran all through our small team, because the Ensign had not been to that end of the grid for a very long time.

The new-development front tires were than fitted and out I went. Sure enough they felt a lot stiffer and better, and consequently I had oversteer. Mo was convinced stiffening the roll bar would balance the car to allow me to take full advantage of the tires' benefits. I was too impatient, would not listen, and insisted on running the old tires I was familiar with. I eventually qualified 15th and made my Grand Prix debut in front of my home crowd starting beside world champion James Hunt. I was a hero on the day, but to this day I often wonder what would have happened if I'd had enough discipline to not be driven by the stopwatch and instead be driven by the car setup. If the car is set up right, the fast lap times just come. I now believe in my heart if I had been disciplined enough to listen to Mo instead of being driven by the stopwatch, my great grid position could have been even better, which might have prompted Goodyear to give us the better tires at the next race, and the rest of the season might have had a better foundation.

On the other side of this story, one of the most disciplined drivers I have ever seen is Al Unser Jr. He would always concentrate on the ultimate race setup and was always able to resist the temptation to just go fast. Al's discipline, however, often led to him starting deep in the field, but in his heyday on race day he was mighty. At the height of his career, Al Unser Jr. won the Long Beach Grand Prix five times in a row.

Then there is the driver who spends too much time focused on the competition rather than on himself and his personal performance. After they run, the first question you hear from them is, "How fast was the opposition?" When he should be concentrating deeply on his own performance, he is instead distracted by the performance of another. Remember, only expend energies on what you can control, which is your own performance. Forget the rest of the competition, because you can not control them. Your performance is the only part of the equation you can control, and that is the only thing that will affect the final outcome on race weekend. Not focusing on your personal performance can be a major flaw that can be corrected.

So what type of talent do you think you have? Do you see yourself in any of these examples? Do you see your friends or competition in any of these examples? Can you see and understand the driving styles of NASCAR, Formula 1 or Indy Car drivers? Can you see where some flourished in certain environments while others floundered? When you closely examine just what type of talent you were blessed with, and if you are very honest with yourself, you can turn any weakness into a strength, but you must understand how to surround yourself with the right environment. If you do this, you can create a foundation for yourself that will stand tall for the rest of your career. Building that platform is a slow process, but you will have a better chance of a good payback if the foundation blocks are solid.

THREE

TECHNICAL
SETUP KNOWLEDGE

*"It takes just as much time to bolt the wrong
setup on to a race car as it does to bolt on the right one."*

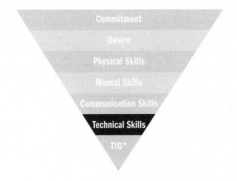

THE MORE KNOWLEDGE engineers acquire about race cars, particularly in spec racing series, the smaller the competitive window becomes within which a driver works, and, more importantly, within which he is judged. It is still my belief the driver who is sharp enough to think deeply enough and make the key accurate small change to his car right before qualifying or a race will more consistently put himself in a position to be more successful than his competition. High performance is still driven by the speed a car can attain, which is dependent upon the fine-tuned setup combination on a car. The best chassis setup contributes to the driver to be positioned to be successful more often than his competition.

You do not have to be a good technical driver to drive a race car fast. However, one of the keys to sustaining championship-winning performances is being a good technical driver. Why, you might ask? Race cars, at whatever level, can go a certain speed. The objective is to get it to a point whereby that maximum speed can be extracted as often as possible. Therefore the key to sustained speed is knowing why the car is fast, not necessarily knowing why the car is slow. Every driver can fairly easily identify why a race car is slow. If a driver (and therefore the team) knows why a race car is fast, he will have a good opportunity to be able to reproduce that speed on a consistent basis.

Ask any driver if he gives good technical feedback and inevitably he will say, "Yes." Drivers like to think they have good technical feedback and they would like others to also have the same opinion. The most successful designer in Formula 1, Adrian Newey, put it succinctly at the end of the 2012 season after his team won a third consecutive driver's and constructor's championship: *"We have a thousand sensors on the car, but ultimately what you really depend on is what the driver says."*

Have you ever noticed that when a driver is tested with a new team, a similar pattern of responses is delivered: "He did a great job and he gave good feedback." Teams love good feedback. It is their lifeblood. It makes their life much easier and it makes the difference between winning and loosing. Remember, it takes just as much time to bolt the wrong setup on to a race car as it does to bolt on the right one. The right setup will ultimately be guided by the driver and by what he says, until they don't believe him.

In the early days of racing, before the advent of contemporary data acquisition, technical feedback from a driver played a much broader role than I believe it does today. What I mean by broader is that without computer help, a driver had to fill in the complete setup picture himself, from suspension to aerodynamics, to engine performance and tire development. In today's world of software, downloading and data acquisition, the driver's feedback direction is just as crucial, but today the driver also has electronic measuring devices that provide him with enormous amounts of data in the graphs and printouts he can use to cross reference his thoughts.

His input is just as valuable, but he now has to work in a much smaller and more precise window, because racing is far more specialized than in the past. This smaller window is also reflected in the grid times of today as opposed to 10 or 15 years ago. When I first raced at the Indianapolis 500 in 1983, the speed spread on the grid, from fastest to slowest, was 207 mph (Teo Fabi) to 183 mph (Chet Fillip), a whopping 24 mph and a time difference of just over 23 seconds over four laps. In 2011 the speed difference was 3.598 mph with a time difference of 2.53 seconds over the four laps of qualifying. When a grid is this close, the emphasis on good and accurate driver feedback becomes even more crucial, because that ultimately determines the setup of the car, which ultimately determines the speed of the car. This clearly shows the window within which drivers and teams now work in is much smaller than in years past. The lesson being you have to be equipped and prepared at a much higher level these days because the margins are razor thin.

Perhaps the most important aspect of car setup and testing is honesty. Honesty endears you to the team and honesty is one of the most important foundation stones in building the rapport with a team, which in turn allows the team to gel. This is also called chemistry between team members. Your instincts and your natural seat-of-the-pants feel will tell you what to say to the engineers (or to your mechanic or helper).

When Derek Daly Performance Driving Academy carried out the Team Green Academy Driver Development program in 1996–1997, we had instances during our evaluations where drivers were talking just for the sake of talking. Because they thought they should be saying something, they would try to show how much they knew instead of just dealing straight with the relevant facts. As soon as a driver begins to force the explanations or goes off on tangents during technical discussions, the engineers' antennas start to go up, and the questions and doubts about his technical skills start to surface.

Never forget a driver's style is unique to him, and therefore his required optimal setup is individual to him. A driver should not be looking to someone else to provide him with his setup. Often in teams when one driver gets lost, another faster driver's setup will be bolted on, and the slower driver will go faster. This is a stop-gap measure for teams and drivers in trouble. In this type of situation, a slower driver will bolt on another driver's setup, but will ultimately fine-tune it to suit his style. Your technical setup should ultimately be directed at suiting your particular driving style. It is fundamentally wrong to try to make a driver change his style to suit a particular car or setup. There are elements of a driver's style that can be shaped differently, but his R-DNA will be tied directly to his natural driving style.

Some cars require a certain technique to make them go fast, but the final tuning of their chassis is individual to every driver. Just look at Michael Schumacher and his many teammates. Many of them tried to change their own styles of driving to mimic his, because whatever he did was considered to be the fastest way. Despite changing their styles, most of his teammates went slower than they would have by sticking to their own style.

Michael Schumacher has always liked his cars predominantly stiffer than that of his teammates. His teammates inevitably get in trouble when they try to use that stiffer setup preferred by Michael. The temptation is, "if it's good for him, it will be good for me." Well, Martin Brundle, Johnny Herbert, Eddie Irvine and Jean Alesi soon found out Michael's setup was designed specifically for him and his style.

It is much harder for some drivers than it is for others to test accurately and to steer a team technically in the right direction. It is always a fine line between seat-of-the-pants speed and chassis feel discipline. In test sessions, a driver should not drive at the limit. What this means is there should always be a little in reserve, because this frees up mental capacity that allows you to concentrate more on what the car is actually doing. If you drive a racing car like a rally car, you will not be an accurate test driver. When you drive at ten tenths, the tendency is to use up all of your concentration abilities just staying on the road. Driving consistently is a vital part of testing. Consistent laps allow you to brake in the same spot each time and use the same lines. When changes are made to the car, they show up easier when a driver is driving consistently. The more talented the driver, the nearer the limit he can drive consistently during a test session.

ROOKIE TENDENCIES

Most rookie race car drivers are not technical drivers and do not give good feedback when they start. When you listen to their explanations about the car, the more they talk the more they get mixed up. Very often, when testing with a new driver (and also with some experienced drivers), after a change is made to the car, he does a run and comes in and completely forgets what he was out there testing. This is a driver who is guided only by the stopwatch. I know this type of driver very well, because I was one of them. I had these tendencies right through Formula 1 and into Champ Cars, and I had to literally talk to myself during test sessions to make sure I did not slip into my instinctive, driven-by-the-stopwatch style.

The good technical drivers tend to also be less emotional. They are much more methodical in their approach and the execution of their job. They are not any slower, just different.

STYLE DIFFERENCES

Style differences are being more and more closely scrutinized these days, again because the window to be competitive is so small. Champ Car champion Paul Tracy had an aggressive style of driving. He was able to perform at his very best when he had a lot of front-end grip. When Bridgestone changed to a harder-compound Champ Car tire in 2001, Paul struggled to find his blinding speed because he could not get the car to respond in the middle of the corners like he wanted it to. When Team Green changed from a Reynard to the Lola for the third round of the 2002 championship in Japan, Tracy immediately topped the time sheets, because the Lola has a much more positive front end, which suited Paul's driving style. The most important thing for Paul, and any engineer that works with him, is to understand what his specific driving style needs to go fast.

Vettel and Webber's style differences literally make the difference between winning and losing, depending on the setup of the car. Mark Hughes contrasted them on Autosport.com: "There's more that's similar than different about the driving styles of the two Red Bull drivers. But the differences there are come mainly in the braking-to-corner-entry phase of a corner. Mark Webber has a great feel for longitudinal grip and can very accurately match how hard he stands on the pedal to what braking grip is available. This is a key skill in that as the down force is on the car at the beginning of the braking phase, you can stand much harder on the pedal without locking the wheels than when the speed comes down.

"A driver therefore has to modulate pedal pressure throughout the braking phase, and the closer you can match the tire's potential without exceeding it, the better. Upon corner entry, Webber likes the car to be stable at the rear so he can commit hard and early on the throttle. Sebastian Vettel isn't quite so extreme in the pedal pressures he generates and sometimes gives a little bit away there at the beginning of a high-speed braking zone, but the differences are small. Where he scores over Webber is in his ease with a rear end that can be lively on corner entry. He's quite relaxed about how the rear will settle down, especially in the power-on phase, and is confident enough to be unperturbed by any wayward transient state between the two phases of the car's behavior."

This is an example of a really small window of performance where the difference in speed is dependent of the setup of the car and the driving style that is attempting to extract the maximum performance from the car. In this case the team listens more to Vettel and attempts to design a car more suited to his rear wayward transient style.

Hughes then described Hamilton and Button as being at opposite ends of the style spectrum, yet driving the same car they make for particularly intriguing comparisons. Button's sensitivity to the car's microbehavior has probably played its part in how the team looks to him more than Hamilton for setup and development direction through a race weekend. Whenever there is a divergence of opinion on Friday over which direction to follow, the team invariably follow Button's preference, probably secure in the knowledge Hamilton will be able to drive well regardless of the car's traits, whereas Button loses more of his performance if the car is not exactly as he needs it. We see also just how sensitivity allows Button to shine in wet, or even better, variably wet conditions

These different styles can require subtle setup differences depending on what a driver's style calls for. Believe it or not, a driver in Formula 1 (Webber) can become uncompetitive compared to his teammate (Vettel) depending on the car's handling tendencies, especially if the rear is a little loose on corner entry.

When young drivers work with driver coaches at their early stages of development, it is imperative the driver coach does not coach a driver to do what the car just can't do—or attempt to get a driver to do what is not symbiotic with his natural style.

GETTING TECHNICALLY LOST

During qualifying for the 1995 Indianapolis 500, the great Team Penske technically fell to pieces. Roger Penske had two of the best drivers at the time in Al Unser Jr. and Emerson Fittipaldi. Fittipaldi's own Penske chassis were just not fast enough to qualify on the first weekend. Every day of the following week Emerson ran as much mileage as possible and still could not coax enough speed from the chassis. In desperation, Roger bought a Reynard from Pagan Racing. Pagan Racing had set the car up to be more than capable of a good qualifying speed with Roberto Guerrero at the wheel. Pagan literally wheeled the car from their garage to Penske's, and Team Penske set about making the car better by rebuilding it and putting their setup on it.

The car never went as fast again. No matter how they tried, Team Penske just could not get enough speed, and to the great embarrassment of Roger, Al Jr., and Emerson, the most successful team in the history of the Indianapolis Motor Speedway failed to get a single car into the race. This was a classic example of too much information, too many engineers and not enough clear direction. Although this type of situation does not happen often, it does happen from time to time, even to the best team in the business.

There is good reason to believe Dale Earnhardt Jr. gets technically lost. His ability to drive a car fast may not be in question, but his ability to continually have his car set up to go fast can be questioned. He is not a consistent performer and this is usually the tipoff he is not technically accurate. *USA Today* columnist Nate Ryan wrote in 2012, "Earnhardt is providing a more businesslike feedback on his car's performance—not unlike the detailed information that helps teammate and five times champion Jimmie Johnson make improvements to the handling of his car." If Jimmie Johnson can accurately adjust his car and make it faster than others, it can become money in the bank as he leaves Earnhardt and others behind.

THE RIGHT WAY

Rick Mears is famous for his methodical approach to races such as the Indianapolis 500. Rick has always said he runs the first 450 miles just to be in a position to run fast and at the front for the last 50 miles. During those 450 miles Rick is constantly feeling what the car does, and more importantly what the car needs on that particular day and in that particular environment and what the car might need to go super-fast during that particular 50 laps.

Over the radio he will give direction to his crew on what he wants changed during the next pit stop. Sometimes he might know what to change and sometimes he will, as accurately as possible, describe the car's symptoms, and he will have his engineer join in the decision making.

During a race the engineer is totally powerless to help unless the driver feeds him accurate information. Can you imagine if the driver fails to read the requirements accurately, and therefore the wrong change is made, or, just as bad no change is made? This does happen, but the great champions, who have a good technical foundation, make more good decisions than bad on average, and this positions them to be more toward the front of the races more often than their competition.

Rick Mears was well known for consistently having the right setup changes made to his cars and hence his place in history as a four-time winner of the greatest racing spectacle in the world, the Indianapolis 500.

Mario Andretti was a great technical driver. There are some who believe his career was prolonged because he was so good technically. He could engineer the car to be faster than most, and therefore the bravery of the younger generation was beaten by the engineering genius of experience. There is no doubt when he won the Formula 1 world championship he was in a car that was faster than everything else on the grid. He was a large part of the reason why the car was faster *because* of his accurate feedback to his engineers. Whether Mario was in a Formula 1 car, an Indy Car, a sports car or a stock car, he could win. This success trait is a hallmark of a good technical driver.

Even rookie Formula 1 drivers can quickly become known as good technical drivers.

Poland's Robert Kubica was credited by BMW for his technical insight and mistake-free pace as major elements that enabled them to develop the BMW in 2006. Even in his short time in Formula 1, he was recognized as a strong technical driver and therefore extremely valuable to a team.

Williams' technical director Sam Michael was instantly impressed by rookie Formula 1 driver Nico Rosberg. Nico's dad, Keke Rosberg, who was my teammate at Williams in 1982 when he won the world championship, was not a good technical driver, but rather he was pure *instinct-reflex*. Nico seems to have a different R-DNA makeup, because he has developed in a different way to his father. After just a short time in Formula 1, Sam Michael said this about Nico:

"I think he can debrief like an engineer. I have not yet worked with a driver able to give detailed analytical feedback as well as Nico."

The other end of the scale for a Formula 1 driver might be former Ferrari driver (and Grand Prix winner) Jean Alesi. Jean was a complete *instinct-reflex* driver with very little technical knowledge. His lack of technical understanding limited his success in Formula 1.

His in-built restrictor (*instinct-reflex talent*) followed him to the German DTM championship after his Formula 1 career ended. On the track he was all entertainment. He could drive a car on the edge of adhesion and almost dare it to fly off the road. He could mesmerize a crowd with his performance. There was a downside to his personal pyramid, such as a lack of understanding of what was going on with the car. His engineers grew frustrated as they were left without accurate technical feedback. AMG technical director Gerhard Ungar once issued an ultimatum to his DTM team at the end of 2005: "He goes or I do." That edict led to Alesi being demoted to an old spec car. This lack of technical understanding was also the reason he did not enjoy that much success in Formula 1 despite his brilliant raw speed.

A crucial moment in Jenson Button's Melbourne 2012 Grand Prix win came when he reconfigured the car on the grid with differential and front wing changes, as he instantly noticed the tires going off just 10 laps into a stint. Had he just let that play out he'd have lost that race. What do you think was the value to McLaren that day in having an accurate technical driver?

Conversely, Kimi Raikkonen would never be expected to be that accurate. His engineers know that and supplement that void as best they can. Undoubtedly this costs performance during a championship run. Kimi has been called a blunt instrument, to whom you could entrust a fast car, but whom you could barely rely on to improve a slow one. In this case the team needs to make sure Kimi is positioned alongside a driver who can bring that missing element. Ferrari did not understand this concept when Raikkonen was paired with Massa and the inevitable happened.

NASCAR crew chief Greg Zipadelli, who led Tony Stewart's team during his successful time at Joe Gibbs Racing when they won two championships, noted that despite his success, Stewart asked to see the setup notes for the car he was about to drive only a couple of times in nine years. This can work as long as you are surrounded by high-caliber, detail-oriented people.

What would you like an engineer to say the about you some day? What choices do you have to make to try to make this possible? Might you be more successful and have more control of your career if you develop into an accurate technical driver? Are you willing to make those choices? Are you willing to make the necessary sacrifices?

How committed are you to being the best you can be in the setup of your car?

LEARNING TECHNICAL SAVVY

None of us are born as good technical drivers with naturally good feedback, as this is a learned trait. Some learn it quickly, while some never learn it at all. Being a good technical driver requires a considerable amount of discipline, because going fast is a driver's natural instinct, yet putting your desire to go fast aside and driving just below the limit with enough mental capacity left to feel the car requires a different mindset. If you are a driver who has a tendency to be driven by what the stopwatch says and not by feel, I urge you to stop right now and consider how much better you would be if you had more discipline and if you worked more diligently on a better setup. A racing car that can go faster will always provide you with an advantage. If you start every race with more of an advantage, you will win more races.

HONESTY

As mentioned earlier, always be brutally honest with the team. If you can't feel a change, then say you can't feel it. Just because they made a change does not mean you will feel it. The worst thing you can do as a driver is to start spewing technical information, fueled by your desire to sound knowledgeable, or by what the stopwatch just told you. This will never develop your weakness and will not endear you to the team. Honesty always has been and always will be one of the most endearing qualities in anyone.

I have seen this trait in many young drivers. Motorsports has a habit of flushing everything out of everybody. It is such a challenging sport, physically, mentally, emotionally and intellectually, that the truth always comes out. Never try to stand on a shaky platform, never try to be what you are not. It will become stamped in your R-DNA, and every team manager will know about it eventually, because they all talk together.

ENVIRONMENT BENEFITS

Jimmy Vasser once told me he might not be the best driver in the world, but he was pretty damn good. I have always admired Jimmy because he enjoyed himself so much while racing. Jimmy is not regarded as a great technical driver. He can drive a car very fast when it is well setup, but he is not able to consistently steer a team in the right direction technically, which is why his results are so up and down. He was always at his best when he was paired with a teammate who could steer the team technically, such as Alex Zanardi, but Jimmy's great strength is his mental toughness.

When Mo Nunn (the same Mo Nunn I saw in 1965 when he was a driver) was an engineer for Chip Ganassi Racing, mainly concentrating on Zanardi's car, he was asked by Chip to go testing with Jimmy at Portland. Having been a former driver himself, Mo has a good idea how drivers work and he can read how to best handle a situation. During the Portland test, Mo controlled Jimmy's input by only allowing him to do a maximum of three laps at a time. If there were areas of uncertainty, Mo would backtrack with the technical setup of the car to get back to a known quantity baseline.

Controlling the test like this did not allow Jimmy to get sidetracked or be tempted to use the stopwatch as a guide to his decision making. At the end of the test, Jimmy had driven faster than anyone had ever gone at Portland. This was a example of a team recognizing how to best manage a situation, and create the right environment within which the driver flourishes, and the team gets quality answers to what is usually an expensive test session.

Lewis Hamilton was environment specific. Mark Hughes highlighted that Hamilton's McLaren environment eventually became unstable for him: "He's about as predictable and settled as a cat in a bath and that energy is part of what makes things happen for him, in the car and out. It's just what flows through him, and he has little control over it. But within that is a total self-belief.

"He knows that he's the world's fastest driver. That combination of fabulous talent, confidence, volatile temperament and a certain naïve immaturity in believing that's all he needs—that success will surely follow—makes for a combustible package." McLaren was not willing to provide the environment within which he could flourish. Instead they tried to manipulate and control him, which resulted in rebellion.

Many of the greats—Jackie Steward, Niki Lauda, Alain Prost, Michael Schumacher and Fernando Alonso—have taken charge of the environment in which they perform, have been intrinsic in molding it to their needs. Hamilton is not wired up in this way. It can therefore be surmised that without the right supportive environment Hamilton in his mind was forced to leave McLaren. It is believed by many that when Hamilton left McLaren at the end of the 2013 season, he was still devoid of an understanding of human dynamics. In Hamilton's mind, the environment pushed him out. Just think about what it might have been like if the environment was conducive to nurturing him and, additionally, if he had developed into a strong and accurate technical driver when he was teenager. He might just be unbeatable.

How many drivers are able to position themselves in an environment that allows them personally to flourish? This is not as easy as it sounds, because most teams are controlled by managers who quite frankly are not open to environment benefits. How many drivers can read their own environment needs accurately, and then have the discipline to slowly try to surround themselves with what they need? Believe it or not, the honesty and openness that comes when a driver admits to a weakness that needs to be supported will go a long way toward creating the necessary environment. A driver's instinct is to go fast. However, speed in a race car is simply a byproduct of having the right components aligned for success more often that the competition.

Tony Kanaan is another very good driver who has shown that his weakness is in the technical department. He has great talent and can win races; however, over the long haul, he has not shown the type of consistent front-running pace of a good technical driver. If Tony (or his manager/coach) had recognized this weakness early in his career and worked harder to turn that weakness into a strength, he would be a much more complete driver today. Tony has many other great strengths, one being his sheer speed in a race car as long as the car is set up to go fast enough. Another would be his ability to mentally process what happens in a race environment, and perhaps Tony's greatest attribute is his desire and commitment to the sport.

Tony Kanaan went on to win the Indy Racing League Championship with some stunning performances; however, it is a well-known fact that Tony's teammates, Brian Herta and Dario Franchitti, were the technical brains behind the teams chassis setup decisions.

This was highlighted at the Indy 500 one afternoon when Franchitti was testing Kanaan's car while Tony watched from the sidelines. When asked why, Tony's reply was that Dario was, *"much more picky than he was."* Therefore the chance to get a better race setup lay in Dario's hands and not his.

In 2011 it's believed that Kanaan strongly suggested that the nineteen-year Formula 1 veteran Rubens Barrichello would be an ideal driver to join the KV IndyCar team that he also drove for because of his strong ability to contribute to the car setup. Tony knew his strengths and weaknesses.

The environment that surrounded Tony during his most successful years at Andretti Green, however, allowed his R-DNA to flourish, because his technically weakness was supported from within the team. I happen to believe that Tony could have been even more successful over the span of his career **if** he had recognized and developed his technical weakness much earlier in his career.

TECHNICAL R-DNA'S

Scott Dixon is an example of a driver who has achieved significant success with some of it coming at a very young age. He currently holds the record for the youngest-ever winner of a CART Champ Car race (20). Dixon was still developing his technical abilities, but even at this stage of his career his reputation of being good technically was beginning to spread. Ganassi Racing's team manager Mike Hull was very open about telling people that Scott knows what the car is doing, and, more importantly, what he needs it to do to suit him at a particular track. He is able to accurately describe these scenarios, which gives his engineers a solid footing when they tune the car. This technical strength that Dixon, and any other good technical drivers have, becomes well known to all interested teams because all teams talk amongst themselves.

Scott Pruett became a good technical driver late in his career. While he was out of Champ Car racing in 1994, Scott was hired by Patrick Racing to spend a season testing and developing Firestone's new Indy Car tires. Scott did 15,000 miles of testing that year, and he admits that testing made him a better driver technically. He was forced to become a disciplined test driver because his feedback would determine what tires Firestone would make for the following season.

It's not a coincidence that some of the great champions are also very accurate technical drivers. The 2005 Formula 1 world champion Fernando Alonso is regarded as a driver with a well-developed technical understanding of a race car.

Pierre Dupasquier is a legend in Formula 1 circles, and for years he was Michelin's competition director, working with some of the sport's greatest drivers. He was an active part of the group that introduced the radial tire to Formula 1 in the late 1970s with Renault, and since then his work with Michelin has brought collaborations with many world champions. All of them made a strong impression on him, and Fernando was no different this year. When it comes to Fernando's work ethic and technical ability, Dupasquier has high praise: "In our job, driver feedback is very important. Fernando has always been very precise in his comments. First of all, he has an incredible memory. He can recall the reference numbers of tires used in a test several months previously! He does the first part of the technical analysis for us, making selections. That is a rare quality."

Perhaps the most direct comment about Alonso's technical ability came from Renault Formula 1 chief designer Tim Densham: "From the design side, he's the ideal driver that you want. When you ask him to test something, you want a black-and-white decision on whether it's better or not. The last thing you want is a driver saying it's better in this corner, but maybe not in that one. Fernando is a positive driver in this, and has always given us straight answers."

Team Penske's Will Power can be regarded as a strong technical driver. Penske team manager Tim Cindric says, "Power is very much like Gil de Ferran with his understanding of the car. He knows how to separate the cars performance from his personal performance. If his engineer asks him about the car, he will not ask for changes until he feels he has extracted the best from himself first.

"He has a very calm demeanor during on track sessions. There is never a panic as he methodically works through each session. When he is qualifying, he has a great ability to execute more mistake-free laps than other drivers. He has a high ability to put it all together when it matters, and when you combine this trait with accurate technical feedback and top-class equipment, you can see how potent the Power Penske partnership can be."

NONTECHNICAL R-DNA

One of the more fascinating stars is former McLaren driver Juan Montoya. He burst on the Formula 1 scene after winning the Indy 500 and the CART Champ Car championship, and was initially hailed as the next Michael Schumacher. Montoya never learned the technical side of a race car and was not able to sustain his winning ability in Formula 1, nor has he become a championship threat in NASCAR.

Montoya's deficiency in the technical department is obvious to the people who know what to look for, yet Juan himself will deny the suggestion and attempt to place the blame for lack of performance elsewhere.

"Juan is one of the most talented drivers I have ever seen; his car control is brilliant and so is his overtaking," former Ferrari driver and manager of the BMW Formula 1 program Gerhard Berger enthuses. "There is nothing to say about this area; he can do the same as Michael on the driving side. I think it's a question of how he can get the maximum out of his car's setup. That's where he is lacking a bit of experience and has to work harder. It's the only area I can think of where he could improve. Maybe he can't."

Remember, motor racing flushes out all the strengths and weaknesses.

"You always need to get the maximum out of the car, but what Gerhard has said is completely the opposite to the others who are saying that I'm going too fast with the car and going too hard," says Montoya.

Montoya continues, "I think the engineers are going to have to push themselves very hard. It's up to them and us to really go through everything with the car to find its sweet spot.

"I'm happy with the way I'm driving. I always try and maximize every lap I do. If I don't know how to maximize the car, then how did I put it on pole position seven times when it wasn't 100 percent capable of it?

"Put simply, we were missing a quicker car."

Despite Montoya's obvious annoyance at the above suggestions, the bottom line here was that when he drove for Williams, neither he nor his teammate Ralf Schumacher were technically accurate enough to develop the car, and therefore the team's overall performance suffered. Montoya is a great example of an *instinct-reflex* driver who can drive the wheels off a car. But you better be able to give him the setup he needs rather than rely upon him to work out what he needs. His golden opportunity to become a champion was presented to him when he was signed by McLaren Mercedes. They are one of the few teams equipped with enough engineering talent on the pit wall to support an *instinct-reflex* driver such as Montoya. However, despite McLaren being enamored with Montoya enough to sign him to a contract, they immediately began to recognize his technical weakness and also questioned his level of dedication and commitment. If the high-water mark for a Champion's Pyramid had already been set by Michael Schumacher or Sebastian Vettel, you need to be at least start at their level to stand a chance of beating them consistently.

When Montoya drove for Chip Ganassi in the CART FedEx championship, he relied totally on his brilliant instincts and reflexes. His engineer was Mo Nunn, who had won championships with drivers such as Mario Andretti, Emerson Fittipaldi and Alex Zanardi. Mo realized quickly that compared to Zanardi, Montoya had little knowledge or interest in the technical side of the race car. Montoya's weakness has been largely masked by his phenomenal instincts and reflexes as he rose through the lower formulae. He was fast, spectacular, and winning races. However, although he was regarded by some as one of the fastest men in Formula 1, his struggles with the BMW Williams team began to highlight his technical weakness. Once at the top of the tree and racing against some of the world's best drivers, he needed more than just his brilliant instincts and reflexes.

After the 2002 United States Grand Prix, Williams BMW co-owner and technical director Patrick Head is on record saying that Montoya needs to up his game if he is to become a champion.

Sam Michael, the then Williams chief operations engineer, expanded on that: "Both our drivers [Montoya and Ralf Schumacher] are certainly capable of being world champions. But they're the same as everyone else in the team in that they need to work harder. It's amazing how much difference a driver can make to the team's motivation—engineers, mechanics, designers and those at the factory. And maybe that's the difference between our two drivers—and I'm not just pointing the finger here, I think it applies to the rest of the grid too—and the best driver, who is Michael Schumacher.

"You hear stories of Michael phoning up [Ferrari sporting director] Jean Todt at 10 o'clock at night and asking about what spring [Luca] Badoer had on this particular lap as he's been looking at the data and there was a lap where he was very quick. Our guys just don't do that."

And what do you think the drivers said after comments like these? Ralf Schumacher defended himself, saying, "I find it strange that so many people assume to know exactly how Michael works. I've always thought I had a pretty good insight into that and I'd be very surprised if Michael would take time away from his family to phone the factory at 10 at night. Getting the best out of yourself is not about phoning the factory at night. Besides, if I phoned Williams at that time, there would be no one there."

Montoya said, "I'm tired of hearing all this bullshit about Michael. If we'd had a car as good as his last year, I think we could have won the championship."

What Montoya misses here is that Michael Schumacher had a car as good as it was because he drove the team technically in the right direction and they therefore built a better car.

Sam Michael comes back with, "Yes, you can say as long as you've got a car with 5 percent more downforce or 20 more horsepower you don't need that extra effort. But the game's too tight not to do it now. Everyone is so close. So if a driver goes to make that final bit of effort, like Michael does, it makes a big difference."

Montoya is a brilliant driver. However, life became more difficult when his competition became Michael Schumacher, Kimi Raikkonen and Fernando Alonso. To beat those three, you need a driver fully developed in all areas, particularly the technical side. It is now apparent that during Montoya's formative years, no series or team taught him the technical side of a race car. This can easily happen, because his blinding speed kept him winning races. Can you imagine if Montoya (or someone close to him or a driver coach) had recognized his weakness earlier in his career? If he was a better driver technically, he could have driven the Williams team to develop a better car. Armed with a better car, I have no doubt he would then have a far greater chance of toppling Michael Schumacher, or any other driver in the world.

For me, it was fascinating to watch the Montoya development play out to see if he could become a more complete driver. He never did, and therefore was run out of Formula 1. American NASCAR racing became his next move and the same strengths and weaknesses went along with him. Again, his weakness became apparent, and although he was able to win the odd race, he never became a championship threat. He never improved technically, and therefore will never be a championship potential winner in NASCAR. If

Jimmie Johnson, for example, can consistently adjust his car to be 0.03 second faster per lap than Montoya, it's game over each Sunday. What usually happens to drivers in this predicament is they move to other teams seeking the type of success that Michael Schumacher or Jeff Gordon have enjoyed before their career eventually ends.

Before he left for McLaren, Sam Michael spent time at Williams, where Rubens Barrichello saw out the last chapter of his Formula 1 career. Michael described Rubens as the missing link in the team, while veteran engineering director Patrick Head reckoned him to be the best development driver Williams had since Damon Hill left at the end of 1996. Add to that his importance in helping Cosworth catch up on the three years of running knowledge it missed during its F1 hiatus, and you have an excellent season's work.

Unfortunately Barrichello did not enjoy the fruits of his quality input, as he was out of Formula 1 when Williams F1 ran their new car in 2012. Pastor Maldonado used it to win the Spanish Grand Prix in Barcelona. How much was that quality input worth to the Williams F1 team?

Being contrasted to Michael Schumacher's work ethic has frustrated many drivers. Consider what one of Michael Schumacher's data engineers Andrea Stella said about his work ethic and technical abilities:

"Most of our solutions come from discussion within the team and that is a very enjoyable way of working. Michael has a very good understanding of the car and this makes our life much easier in a way, because he can give you not only the feeling he has from actually driving the car, but also the feeling on which direction we should go in terms of setting up the car. In fact, I think he could almost engineer his own car!"

That's not to say Montoya could not have become a world champion (if he had the desire and commitment), because other nontechnical drivers who have won major championships are Keke Rosberg, Mika Hakkinen, Jimmy Vasser and Lewis Hamilton. In the case of Hamilton, he has been able to win Grands Prix and became the F1 world champion. In *Autosport* it was stated that, "Technical feedback has been something of a weakness throughout Hamilton's whole career. He often goes down blind alleys and has a tendency to follow where his driving instincts take him."

So, given his a nontechnical R-DNA, how did Hamilton manage to win races and a world championship? Hamilton was quoted in *Motorsport* as saying, "When you do finally get the package underneath you, then there is obviously an optimal setting which helps you drive the car to the limit. When it comes to that, some drivers are able to extract more from their engineers, their cars, than others."

This may be true in the short term, but history has shown that sustained great performances only come when all the skills needed are developed and active. Without strong technical abilities, a driver's success is placed in other people's hands. With Hamilton's move from McLaren to Mercedes for 2013, he will rely heavily on the technical ability of his teammate Nico Rosberg, and he will have to hope Rosberg has at least the same technical ability as Jenson Button, and that the engineering team at Mercedes can provide a fast car for him even if overall driver feedback is not optimum.

HOW TO BECOME A BETTER TECHNICAL DRIVER

Going faster is not just about driving better, it's about having a better car.

Now that you know what you need to do, you now need to learn how to do it. The first question I want to ask is this: Knowing that human beings shy away from their weaknesses, are you prepared to make the commitment necessary to do whatever it takes to become a better technical driver? If the answer, and therefore your choice, is a wholehearted, "Yes," then you have at least a fighting chance, and because of the fact that it might not be a strength of yours, make no mistake about it, it will be hard work. You need to mentally decide whether the end result will be worth it or not. That's right, this is also a test of your desire to be the best you can be.

YOUR RESPONSIBILITY

There is no shortcut to learning the technical side of a race car. You cannot learn it from a book, video or from behind a desk. You will only learn it by experiencing it. Make every lap you do count. Get a notepad, write everything down and study what it all means. Then get into the habit of taking copies of all setups used on your race car. Get a copy of all software used for the data capture on the race car and load it onto your laptop. Then follow through on your personal commitment and go back to school and begin to study.

For the *instinct-reflex* driver, this aspect of the job can be somewhat difficult. In addition to studying and gaining a practical understanding of the technical changes, he also has to develop the discipline to drive the car in a more consistent way and not at 10/10ths all the time. It is a very natural thing for an *instinct-reflex* driver to just drive flat-out; that's what we love about them. It's also a short-term benefit to the team, because the stopwatch makes them smile. However, for the driver, he has just spent a day proving he has great speed over a lap (which we already knew), but he lost the opportunity to further develop the car and the Champion's Pyramid.

THE FORMATIVE YEARS

At as early an age as possible, whoever your mechanic is (dad, paid help, friend, whomever) should be required to discuss all technical changes with you prior to changing the car. Whether you are racing a go-kart, Midget, Formula Ford or whatever, make it your responsibility to learn what is going on. The glory is in going fast, but there will not be a consistent payback of glory days if you are relying on others to create your ideal environment for you. You have a personal responsibility to yourself to understand and control your technical environment.

Make yourself ask questions about the setup. There is no such thing as a stupid question. When changes are made to the car, insist on understanding why and how it affected the car. Never be afraid to ask the mechanics or engineers why or how. They will be delighted to explain it to you, because they know the better you understand the setup, the more you will help them and the faster the car will go.

Whenever you go to a test, the team will keep a log of every comment, every lap time and every change. Make sure you get a copy of this report as soon as you can and study it until you have a very clear picture of what happened and why it happened. If it helps you, add your own personal notes that will help you recall what happened if you need to reference the notes at a later time.

When you go home, pull out your setup sheets for the test sessions and go over them lap by lap and change by change. People generally shy away from what they don't know, and it's the same with engineering a car. However, the more you study and apply yourself to learning about the car technically, the easier it will be for you to understand the technical side of it and the more likely you will be to immerse yourself in it.

How many people do you know who would not buy a computer because they knew nothing about it? After a few months suddenly they are sending e-mails, surfing the web, downloading apps and realize that they can no longer live without it. There is a fear of the unknown, so become familiar with the unknown as soon as possible, and it will pay you dividends in results and, in turn, financially.

STAY ON TRACK

British star Jenson Button learned some lessons the hard way when he raced in Formula 1 for the first time. He was too casual and did not think enough about what he was doing. He was caught up in the flash and dazzle of F1. He spent more time with his girlfriends than with his engineers. He did realize it, though, before it became too late.

"In the early part of last year, it's probably true that I didn't spend enough time with the engineers attending to detail," says Button.

It was partly attitude, partly inexperience. The car was initially so fundamentally bad, he didn't know where to start, didn't have the hard points of reference.

"I am able to do more now than I was then," he says. "I can relate to the engineers, whereas before I was, 'What's that all about?' I'm definitely able to put in more hours now."

In an earlier chapter I mentioned relationships and friendships are what drive motorsports. Team managers and associates talk all the time about drivers and their good and bad points. While a team might not slam a driver, if his weakness is technical, that trait becomes known to everyone. Remember what I said earlier, that the truth is the only thing that does not change and you can't hide the truth forever, hence the need to recognize at an early stage your strength and weaknesses and make sure you turn any weaknesses into a strength. A good technical driver means any investment in new developments for a car becomes money well spent. Likewise if a driver gives inaccurate technical feedback, a chunk of the team's budget might easily be wasted, which can lead to finger pointing, which can alienate the driver from the team.

Learning the technical side is not part of the glamorous side of racing. A mechanic having to clean up dirty oil from a crashed oil tank is not glamorous either. However, just like all good mechanics, the driving force that makes you work through the difficult times is the mental picture of you standing on the victory podium celebrating a job well done.

However, I will caution drivers and parents that it has been my experience that drivers have to reach a certain age to be able to really process and understand this type of technical information. Drivers younger then 14 will have a difficult time doing this. This does not mean you should not bother with it if your child is younger than 14. He still must get into the habit of having the right work ethic, which lays the foundation for him to learn at a much faster rate when he begins to be able to process the information (and hence retain) at a much faster rate.

Between 14 and 17 is when the floodgates open with most drivers and they begin to process information a lot faster and it all begins to make sense. Telling a driver what it does is not as good as the driver discovering for himself what it does. Experiential learning is the most powerful of all and is summed up by the adage, "Show me, don't tell me." The race car shows the drivers what happens with different chassis settings. Sometimes this experiential learning will be remembered for a lifetime.

FOUR

COMMUNICATIONS

"There is no such thing as reality, only perception."

DURING THE TEAM GREEN ACADEMY driver development program in 1996–1997, we put many of the drivers through a basic communications course. None of the drivers had ever attended a course like this before. Almost everyone, each young driver said, "If only I had known this information last season," because they could all relate to friction within a team that could have been dealt with differently and more effectively.

Have you ever seen the advertisement from Chester Karras in the in-flight magazines where it says, "You don't get what you deserve, you get what you negotiate." Well the same could be true for a racing driver. You get what you negotiate by way of your ability to communicate. You could be the most gifted driver who ever walked the face of the earth, but if you can't use the power of communications to get yourself into the environment that could allow you to shine, you, your friends and your mom and dad may be the only ones fully aware of your talent.

The dictionary lists communication as the exchange of thoughts, messages or information, by speech, signals, writing or behavior. This is verbal communication, but there is also body language. Body language is what emanates from you, it's a language all of its own and it can be a persuasive language of confidence. It can also be a hindrance to a driver if the body language portrays a lack of confidence or a weakness. When someone looks you in the eye during a handshake, there is a connection that can carry sincerity with it. There is a confidence exuded from a driver when he boldly communicates verbally and with body language. A trust can be built quickly with good verbal and body language communications.

The opposite is a driver who looks lost or unsure of himself when meeting someone new. If the handshake is weak, if the eyes wander or if the shoulders are stooped, confidence would not be instilled to the recipient. If the recipient senses the driver has a lack of confidence, it becomes harder to prove your worth and value as a driver. Body language is power and it can be used to open or close doors. People will embrace others they feel they can trust, and trust is built through effective communications.

Something interesting happened when my son Conor at fourteen years of age first met Australian Formula 1 driver Mark Webber. After the initial handshake, Mark immediately placed his left hand on Conor's lower back and his other hand pushed his upper chest to a more upright position. As he did this, he said to him that he should carry himself in a more upright and proud manner because it exudes more confidence. Mark is well known for his physical fitness exploits outside the cockpit and he is a great believer that your physical self is a reflection of your mental and emotional self. He therefore likes to see young drivers exude a confident look and feel that says, "I have the ability, the strengths and I know where I'm going." Mark even commented on Conor's feet positioning. Conor had a toe out look and Mark is a believer that the feet pointed straight ahead helped the body be more aligned and therefore move in the right direction.

Good communications, both verbal and physical, can help create the racing environment you need to be successful. The opposite is also true; poor communications is just not as effective. Good communications can be as simple as an e-mail update, a verbal affirmation, a handshake, a nod or a wink, and most of all supportive behavior both on and off the track. I'm sure you have heard the old adage that perception is reality. I would go a little further and say there is no such thing as reality, only perception. What perception do you want to give?

The first time I heard the phrase, "There is no such thing as reality, only perception," I was a little perplexed. Then I thought hard about it and began to realize that maybe it means that what is truth to one, is different than what is truth to another. A more accurate use of this phrase might be: "There is no such thing as reality, just your personal perception of what that reality might be." Your perspective then determines your emotional response.

Everybody lives in their own world and sees and interprets their reality through their perception. What we term as reality is in fact different for everyone. Everyone interprets each situation according to how they personally process information. When you consider how you communicate, you have to allow for the fact everyone processes information differently and everyone interprets circumstances differently. Its not unusual for people to start to get a little glassy-eyed when I discuss this subject, but the longer and deeper you think about it, the more you will see what a difference it can make when you communicate effectively with people.

Communications covers a broad spectrum that includes verbal skills, people skills, body language and situational awareness skills. The first thing any driver needs to fully understand about communications is that motor racing is a team sport. Therefore you have to communicate, recognize and appreciate all team members. The well-known phrase "Sticks and stones may break my bones, but words will never hurt me," I believe can be 100 percent wrong. If you are guilty of verbal abuse of any of your team members, I promise you may live to regret ever saying it. Despite the short-term personal satisfaction of blurting out your one-sided story, you will seldom benefit from any type of emotional outburst.

Communication is your direct connection to your team. Good communications keeps you plugged into your team and keeps them on your side. Drivers have the power to control this.

TEMPERAMENTS AND PERSONALITIES

Most people in a motor racing paddock have no idea about the following information. However, after reading the original *Race to Win*, I had Indy 500 drivers call me to say the temperaments chapter revolutionized how they communicate within their families and their business associates.

From the beginning of time, it has been common knowledge people are different in every possible way. They are different in their background, their upbringing and their physical appearance. In this chapter I will focus on the four basic temperaments that shape who you are as a person and how you interact with the others. This chapter has the potential to revolutionize how you communicate with others through your unique style. It is your individual style of seeing, and, more importantly, communicating with the world around you and having a basic understanding of the temperaments that can have a profound impact when dealing with your team, your family and your business.

There are four primary temperaments, and, like blood types, they never change. Each come with their own set of strengths and weaknesses and characteristics you will be able to discern, and therefore assist you in navigating your way through conversations and conflicts with a better understanding of all points of view, and therefore a greater opportunity for a quicker resolution.

As a side note, a majority of corporations, large and small, give personality tests to applicants during the hiring process to make sure the individual fits the position being sought. It is an invaluable resource for studying behaviors and why people respond the way they do. It is also interesting to note that until I understood the four different types, I assumed everybody viewed life, or should, from my view. Can you begin to see the potential for conflict? One more thing, it is very common to be a blend of another temperament. In other words, you will have a primary and a secondary blend of temperaments, but your primary will always be dominant. As you read and understand this information, you will begin to categorize your friends, teammates and team leaders, and you will have a deeper understanding of how and why they communicate the way they do. You will also learn how to better walk through their door of communication and be a stronger group because of it.

THE FOUR BASIC TEMPERAMENTS

The original Greek names are Choleric, Sanguine, Phlegmatic and Melancholy. Please remember a temperament is not right or wrong, just different. Everyone has a dominant temperament and it will be blended with a secondary.

CHOLERIC: "THE DOER"

This temperament is task- and result-oriented. These people possess strong leadership skills and are very driven. Making friends is not their priority, getting the job done is. They would appear be somewhat aggressive, assertive, almost abrasive. They usually end up in a management role because of their ability to get all the tasks done.

SANGUINE: "THE TALKER"

This temperament is fun, extroverted, outgoing and colorful party people. They usually have a lot of friends. Life is all about adventure, excitement and being active, engaged and stimulated. They laugh and talk a lot, and are fun people to be around. You can usually find these outgoing people in public relations, sales and marketing.

PHLEGMATIC: "THE WATCHER"

This temperament is the most likable of all four types. They are easygoing, nonoffensive, and loyal types, and are usually good followers and good listeners. They would be somewhat people-centered, romantics, family-oriented types who like togetherness. If they were an animal, they would be a golden retriever. Sometimes appear indifferent and apathetic. But never mistake their style for weakness.

MELANCHOLY: "THE THINKER"

This is the deep-thinker temperament, who is very black-and-white, extremely analytical and can often appear to be moody. They can be visionaries, perfectionists, people who love charts, graphs and facts. These would be race team engineers, statisticians, math gurus, doctors and accountants.

To give you an idea of the words that might describe the four temperaments, consider the table below:

CHOLORIC	SANGUINE	PHLEGMATIC	MELANCHOLY
Bottom line	Thrill	Honest feelings	Imagine
Duty	Imagine	Sympathy	Cautious
Law-abiding	Games	Sharing	Inner experience
Dependable	Stir the blood	Brotherly love	Foresight
Obedient	Fast machines	Heart	Intuition
Structured	Light-hearted	Harmony	Mystery
Status	Performer	Hug	Caring
Power	Jokes	Friendly	Reasonable
Control	Good time	Concern from	Creative
Track record	Danger	the bottom of one's heart	Science-fiction
			New and better ways

Now let's look at what behaviors they each might exhibit.

When you consider the above temperaments, the majority of the population has at least two different temperaments operating at any given time. But it would be rare, if ever, to have your opposite as a blend. For example, you could have an analytical (Melancholy) race engineer who has a driven (Choleric) or easygoing (Phlegmatic) blend, but would be very rare to have a life of the party (Sanguine) as a secondary.

Consider this: What if you were working with your race engineer (Melancholy) and he was very data-driven laptop engineer? His communication style therefore requires you to sit down for an hour after each session and accurately discuss in minute detail every aspect of the chassis, engine, gearbox and race track. He would probably also want you to pore over data graphs in fine detail in an effort to provide him with as much information as possible. It is his job then to take all that information and have it make sense and use it to help the car go faster. If you are a driver who does not like to get bogged down with the details, and if you walk in and simply tell him it oversteers and you're off to play golf, the chances are you will not have connected with him, nor will you have satisfied his requirements. This would be an ineffective way to communicate with your engineer.

On the other hand, if your race engineer is what I call a trench engineer, and all he needs to know is the very basics of the problem with the car, and you want to sit down for an hour with him and explain every aspect in minute detail, and ask him to spend hours studying data graph, again you will not have connected with him nor satisfied his requirements.

If you had the skills to be able to read what type of person you are dealing with, don't you think that might give you a head start to having effective communications with the people who matter on your teams? Absolutely it would.

The real key to effective communications is three-fold: how to project your own personality and wishes in a supportive way, how to recognize the personalities of the people you are dealing with and how to communicate most effectively with them.

The table on pages 120–121 will give you the clues you need when learning to read what type of personalities you are dealing with.

Now you have learned how to read the personalities you are dealing with, the table on pages 122–123 will help you understand how to communicate more effectively with them.

So now let's deal with you. Which category do you fit in? What type of personality would be your dominant and what would be your secondary personality trait? As a first test look at your parents and decide what their temperaments are. Do they appear to be opposites? Bear in mind a personality trait is like your blood type; you have it for life and you can't change it, and whatever one you have will bring with it strengths and weaknesses. You can't change your temperament, but you can make sure your weaknesses do not become a hindrance to you and get in the way of effective communication and relationships.

The graph on page 124 is a great reference tool. Study it and you will see clearly the pattern of behavior for everyone you know. For example, if you look at the right side of center, you will notice the Choleric/Sanguine combinations are direct, extrovert talkers. Conversely the left side of center, the Melancholy/Phlegmatic blend is more of the introverted, deep-thinking, less-confrontational types.

Over the years I have had to temper my Choleric style. My aggressive and sometimes abrupt style very often did not lay a good foundation for constructive communications. My one-track mind during my early career right up through Formula 1 was not conducive to professional relationship-building, which would have greatly helped me at the time. As the old adage goes, "I wish I knew then what I know now,

BEHAVIOR	**CHOLERIC (Doer)**	**SANGUINE (Talker)**
CHARACTERISTICS/ STRENGTHS	Go-getters, ambitious	Networkers, socializers
WHAT THEY TALK ABOUT	I will ... results, what they want to achieve. Talks objectively. Avoids small talk.	
WAY THEY TALK	States commands, direct assertion, commands	States commands, direct assertion
TONE OF SPEECH	Louder, uses voice to emphasize points	Louder, gets easily excited, uses voice to emphasize
PACE OF SPEECH	Fast	Fast
BODY LANGUAGE	Leans forward, limited or no facial expressions. Intense eye contact, deliberate movements	Leans forward, controlled facial expressions, good eye contact, lots of gestures
COMMUNICATION STYLE	Direct, to the point, can be outspoken, formal, businesslike	Animated, excitable, can come on too strong, informal, casual
RESPONSIVENESS	May appear pushy, more reserved and cautious, can appear preoccupied	Open and warm, animated, enthusiastic, enjoys the conversation
LISTENING PATTERN	Can be a poor listener, wants to control conversation. May interrupt, likes to summarize.	Listens, reacts to what you are saying, talks a lot
MOTIVATED BY	Results	Applause
THRIVES ON	Pressure, change	Stimulation, fun
EXPRESSION OF ANGER	Impatient, aggressive	Easily frustrated, can be explosive
WORK STYLE	Works in priority order, makes priority lists, does several things at once, intense, driven	Unstructured, likes freedom, lots of people interaction, makes lists of people to call and places to go
WORK AREA	Functional, organized. Work is in priority order.	Interesting things, gadgets, novelty items, give always readily displayed

PHLEGMATIC (Watcher)	MELANCHOLY (Thinker)
Peacemakers, bridge-builders	Fact-finders, pragmatists
I feel, feelings, shares personal feelings	I think, numbers, facts, talks objectively, avoids small talk
Inquires, indirect assertion	Inquires, unimposing
Quieter, does not vary voice much	Quieter, does not vary voice much
Slower	Moderate
Leans back, some facial expressions, good eye contact, uses gestures	Leans back, limited or no facial expressions, limited eye contact, limited gestures
Dreamy thoughts, may seem vague, informal, casual	Specific, concise, clear, logical, formal, bottom line
Friendly, responsive, enjoys the conversation	May appear unresponsive, reserved and cautious, can appear preoccupied
Good listener, reacts to what you are saying, cares	Listens, but may appear they are not
Approval	Activity
Togetherness, support	Accuracy, information
Gentle, gets flustered	Slow to anger, rational approach
Easygoing, cooperative, always willing to be of service, goes with the flow, no strong sense of urgency	Thorough, attentive to detail, step-by-step procedures, works in sequence, to-do lists, one thing at a time, pensive
Sentimental mementos and souvenirs, pictures of family and friends, desk may appear cluttered	References are at fingertips, lots of paper, work is in piles

Now that you have learned how to read the personalities you are dealing with, the following table will help you understand how to communicate more effectively with them.

CHOLERIC	SANGUINE
IMPATIENT. Be more patient, give myself a longer lead time, be more tolerant of delays, relax	LIKES TO WORK IN UNSTRUCTURED WAY. Be more organized, let others organize me, pay more attention to details
PRESSURES OTHERS. Slow down, pressure others less, be sensitive to others' needs, take on less, be aware of my own limitations	COMES ON STRONG. Be careful not to intimidate others, don't steal too much of the limelight
COMPETITIVE SPIRIT. Remember, I'm part of a team, results will speak for themselves, avoid being too independent	REACTS EMOTIONALLY. Avoid embellishments and exaggerations, take time before I react, state my case objectively
LIKES TO BE IN CONTROL. Let others take control, volunteer less, avoid playing power politics	INTERESTED IN EVERYONE AND EVERYTHING. Get down to business quicker, try not to get overly involved with people
INTERRUPTS. Let people complete their sentences, take a breath before I respond	TALKS A LOT. Don't dominate the conversation, ask open-ended questions of others
SETS MANY GOALS. Limit the number of goals I set, focus on results	GOALS MAY KILL SPONTANEITY. Be spontaneous about means to reach goals, reach my goals by telling others

and how different things might have been." The reality is what's behind and past is only a benefit if I learned from it.

Many people would like to be a Sanguine, because they love life and people love them because they can be very entertaining and fun at parties. However, sometimes they have difficulty convincing team managers they are serious about their craft. A Sanguine would be Helio Castroneves,

PHLEGMATIC	MELANCHOLY
SLOW PACE. Avoid being too slow, set deadlines, don't get overwhelmed by pressure	FOCUSES ON FACTS AND FIGURES. Reduce reliance on facts alone, use other information, trust my intuition
APPEARS VAGUE. Think before I speak, organize my thoughts	MORE TASK- THAN PEOPLE-ORIENTED. Develop relationships, avoid being judgmental
GETS PERSONALLY INVOLVED. Leave home issues at home, don't get too close to coworkers, be more private	REMAINS OBJECTIVE. Share my feelings, avoid being aloof, come to a decision quicker
KEEPS THE PEACE. Don't be afraid to take a stance, assert myself more, take the initiative	SOMEWHAT INFLEXIBLE. Change plans and deadlines accordingly, be less of a perfectionist, allow others to communicate in their own way
SOMETIMES DOESN'T SPEAK UP. State my opinion—it's important	USUALLY LISTENS, BUT WE WOULDN'T KNOW IT. Nonverbally show I am listening, be more spontaneous
CAUTIOUS ABOUT COMMITMENT TO GOALS. Achieve goals with someone else, take action quicker	GOALS MUST BE MET ON TIME. Goals and deadlines may need to be changed, be flexible about my deadlines

Tony Kanaan, Gerhard Berger, Jean Alesi. Are you a Sanguine? If Sanguine is your dominant, what do you think your blend (secondary) would be?

Vettel is a Choleric but his blend is Sanguine. He's a lot of fun and has a very well developed sense of humor, yet fiercely competitive and results-oriented. Mark Hughes thinks he's the most abstract-intelligent of all the drivers—by far. He

TEMPERAMENTS

DELIBERATE
(Task-oriented)

MELANCHOLY
(Thinker)

CHOLERIC
(Doer)

INDIRECT
(Introvert)

DIRECT
(Extrovert)

Opposite

Opposite

PHLEGMATIC
(Watcher)

SANGUINE
(Talker)

SPONTANEOUS
(People-oriented)

has a wide comprehension of all sorts of disciplines, a great interest and knowledge of history and culture, but combined with boy next door cheekiness. But in competition mode he's a savage animal.

Dario Franchitti might be your Melancholy/Phlegmatic blend because of his desire for neatness—his seat has to fit just perfectly, his driving suit has to be just right—but his easygoing style is a typical Phlegmatic trait. Melancholies do not like dramatic change and they like to talk facts. Dario needs an engineer who is a straight-shooter, yet emotionally supportive.

Nigel Mansell might be a good example of a Choleric. He was black-and-white, aggressive, in your face, my way or the highway. Mansell did not make a lot of friends and he needed a strong-minded engineer who was not easily intimidated. If Mansell respects you, he will follow you. He did not need any emotional support from the team to perform well. In fact he thrived in hostile environments where he reveled in proving how good he was.

Will Power might be another good example of a Choleric. The tipoff is he is forever asking questions. He can also be prone to emotional outbursts. Remember the emotionally laden two-finger salute to race control in New Hampshire in 2011 when the race was restarted in spite of the rain falling. There was a big crash that involved him and he let his thoughts be known in full view of the television cameras. Yes, Cholerics are prone to be emotionally driven and spontaneous. A Phlegmatic would never do this.

A.J. Foyt was like this—Choleric. All through his career people knew it was Foyt's way or no way. Even when he retired and ran his own teams, he still insisted on doing things his way. He was famous for his outbursts when things did not go his way. He almost endeared himself to people with his outbursts. Unfortunately his way was the old way, and the modern world is much more structured and organized, and without a more rigid structure of planning and executing, the old-school teams can get left behind.

Jimmy Vasser would be a Phlegmatic. He is easygoing, does not rock the boat and will not cause trouble in the team. His engineer needs to be strong-willed to make sure he steers Jimmy the right way.

2006 Indy 500 winner Sam Hornish would also be in this category. Sam is supremely gifted as a driver, but outside the cockpit his world moves a lot slower than most. He does not rock the boat, is very compliant to the wishes of others, and will go with the flow rather than rock the boat.

Mario Andretti would be a Phlegmatic. Part of Mario's charm is his slow speech delivery, his easy, measured moves at events and his generally relational demeanor. As tough as he was in a race car, he is almost the opposite without his helmet on.

As I continue to learn more and more about different temperaments, I can confidently tell you a Phlegmatic temperament is one of the most liked within a team, and in everyday life as well, because they are so relational and easygoing by default. I can also tell you I believe there are two types of Phlegmatic: Active and Passive. The Active Phlegmatic can be easygoing (and therefore frustrating to a Choleric), but when he truly wants something, he has the ability to go after it—full-steam ahead. The Passive Phlegmatic is perhaps the hardest temperament to handle during the developmental stages, because he just won't take the initiative. The Passive Phlegmatic needs to be very careful, because the world of motorsports can very easily pass them by as they continue to hope their talent alone will carry them through, which of course in this day and age is a risky route to take.

NASCAR's Michael Waltrip, Kenny Schrader and Kenny Wallace would all have Sanguine as their dominant temperament. Helio Castroneves and Tony Kanaan would also be the Sanguines. Think about their dominant behavior: fun-loving and outgoing.

Jeff Gordon is more of a Choleric and is a good communicator. Whether this is a natural trait or a learned one, I don't know. What I do know is Jeff's ability to communicate and energize people is part of what has made him so successful for so long.

In 1998, NASCAR's most prolific and successful team of Jeff Gordon and his crew chief Ray Evernham were split up when Ray left Hendrick Motorsports to form his own team. Jeff and Ray had won three Winston Cup championships together. Shortly after Ray's departure, Jeff's over-the-wall pit crew, known as the Rainbow Warriors, also left. This is usually a devastating blow to drivers and teams.

At that time, Jeff Gordon could have easily become dejected, and his dejection could have left the ship rudderless. Instead he got behind his new team led by Steve Letarte, and over the course of the following years helped guide and lead them to winning his fourth Winston Cup championship in 2001 with a new group of committed people. He did this through total support, which was demonstrated to them through good communications and supportive behavior. It is no coincidence every time Jeff Gordon is in victory circle the first thing he says is, "Thank you to my team."

In the 2002 Indianapolis 500, Gil de Ferran left the pit lane toward the end of the race and a rear wheel fell off. This undoubtedly cost Gil a win at the biggest racing event in the world. Just think what would happen if Gil had elected to vent his anger and verbally abuse his team for their mistake. I doubt he would have had much support for the rest of the season. Instead he went to each team member, shook their hand and said thank you for their personal efforts and commitments. Gil knows that for the long-term success of his team, and therefore himself, he must always understand people make mistakes, and that success only comes for a driver with the coordinated efforts of teams of people. The following year the same team, who respected and supported their driver, worked flawlessly and Gil de Ferran finally won the world's biggest motorsport event, the Indianapolis 500.

Three-times Formula 1 World Champion Ayrton Senna was a great communicator, and his most effective way of communicating with his team was through touch and verbal affirmation. Every morning upon arrival at the race track, he would shake hands with each of his mechanics, and every evening before he left he would do the same thing. It was his simple and effective way of saying, "Thank you." Every mechanic loved to get the handshake, because, to them, it was an affirmation of friendship and respect for what they were doing.

In 1993 I covered Formula 1 for ESPN, and at the opening race of the season in South Africa I found myself standing outside the McLaren pit waiting to do an interview with Michael Andretti. When Michael's teammate Ayrton

Senna walked through the back door, he recognized me and walked around both of the race cars, zigzagged past half a dozen mechanics, and came straight over to me with his hand outstretched to introduce himself. I had never met Senna before, but like everyone else in motorsports I had admired him. He had become familiar with me through his knowledge of the history of Formula 1 and through his interest in following Indy Car racing on television where I was the commentator.

I was completely floored a multiple world champion, who usually has to hide from fans and admirers, would even bother to take the time to introduce himself to me. That simple gesture of communication had a profound effect upon me.

How well do you know your family, your friends, your coworkers, and your race team members? Knowing their temperament could make or break any relationship within the team or life.

APPROVAL ADDICTS

I know I've mentioned this before, but it's worth noting again for reinforcement. As we move more and more toward vast amounts of knowledge being freely available, we also move more and more toward the window to make it in racing (or any athletic endeavor) being smaller and smaller, and, therefore by definition, more difficult. This is because every hopeful athlete now has the information available to him, and by hard work and dedication even the non-super-gifted athlete can go a long way in the sport without ever having what it really takes to make it to the top. The problem is he will fill a lot of slots along the way (especially if he has financial backing), taking opportunities away from the truly gifted drivers, therefore making it more difficult for the really gifted guy to surface. This is the way of the world today, and we will not change it.

Therefore, as we adapt to the way of the current world, we are forced to develop an elite athlete at a much deeper level, first by understanding him and then by equipping him for the increased needs of the sport. Because mental skills restrict just about every other skill we learn, I have gone deeper than normal with the following explanation. This is deeper than most parents I know understand, and it is a crossover point between mental skills and communications.

Just like there are two different types of driving talents a driver is born with (*instinct-reflex or feel-sensitive*), a driver's behavior and internal motivational push button can also be broken down into two different categories: *internal approval addict* and *external approval addict*. The *internal approval addict* is task-centric, which is Choleric/Melancholy, and the *external approval addict* is people-centric, which is Sanguine/Phlegmatic.

Task-centric people do not need as much external approval, as they are driven more internally and therefore push themselves to succeed more for themselves. Their own personal sense of satisfaction is dominant. People-centric individuals are more relational-oriented and therefore are driven by their relationships outside themselves, and tend to need more approval from their outside world. Their satisfaction comes more from pleasing others.

So here's where this gets interesting. A particular temperament predisposes a driver toward behaving one way or the other. These two different temperament categories—behaviors—of a driver's makeup can exhibit the following different tendencies. The *internal approval addict* does not really care what people think or say. They can forget mistakes more quickly and move to the next area of improvement as quickly as possible because in their mind they are mainly dealing with performing (and pleasing) just one person—themselves.

The *external approval addict*—the people pleaser—can take a lot longer to get over mistakes, because in their mind they touched so many people externally and they care what they think. The more people who know of a mistake, the more people he has to worry about. It's easier to control just one—yourself—than it is to control the masses. It's easier to control what you think than it is to control what they think, and this can be a trap for the Sanguine/Phlegmatic. When you know what you are dealing with and the predispositions that come along with it, it's a coach's job to put the developing athlete in an environment where they can flourish in spite of the ever-changing outside circumstances.

A PERSONAL BLUNDER

In 1981 at the British Grand Prix at Silverstone, I was driving the March Formula 1 car in front of many of my family and friends. The British Grand Prix was always regarded by me as my home race. It was a very emotional event for me and a very important race for me to perform well in. It was an unusual year in Formula 1, because of the legal cheating that went on with artificially raised ride heights in the pit lane. Essentially, each car had to have a certain ride height when measured in the pit lane. That same ride height was supposed to be maintained out on the circuit, but most teams had hydraulic lowering devices fitted to the shock absorber and spring platforms that would allow the car to run lower. This allowed the underbody (which generated most of the downforce) to run lower, which generated more downforce and therefore the car went much faster. My team did not have this lowering device for the first six races and I failed to even qualify for a starting position. I had one of Ireland's best known companies, Guinness, as my primary sponsor for the 1981 season, so there was a huge emotional investment in the British Grand Prix, and I was hoping, deep within my heart, for a good showing.

My chief mechanic, Ray Boulter, was a dedicated worker with a wonderful Cockney accent. He was just as frustrated as I was we had failed to qualify in the first six races of the season.

Before the first practice session as we talked loosely in the garages, Ray was having some good lighthearted fun at my

Derek began his career as a race car driver in a 1952 Ford Anglia E93A. This photo was taken in 1969, when he was 16 years old.

Very quickly Derek established himself as a winner, especially driving his Mini Cooper.

Derek won two championships in a Mini and is shown here in 1972.

Derek Daly and his mentor Derek "Big D" McMahon during the 1977 Formula 3 season.

Formula Ford in England was cut throat in 1976. Derek won 23 races in a Hawke DL15/17.

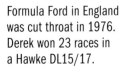

Team owner Mo Nunn advises Derek (in the Ensign Formula 1 car) during the 1978 Formula 1 season.

Ensign in Argentina—instead of having the discipline and focus on making the setup better, Derek was more focused on trying to drive it faster.

Derek drove for Williams in 1982 and almost won the Grand Prix of Monaco.

The last time Derek competed in Daytona (1992) he put the Nissan on the pole.

Instead of working out, 1982 world champion Keke Rosberg made helmet tie straps that attached to the side of the cockpit to support his head.

Derek and Mario Andretti share a light-hearted moment.

Derek and Andretti have remained close over the years and are regular contributors to the Indy 500 broadcast.

Derek interviews Jackie Stewart on the grid of the U.S. Grand Prix. Jackie was one the first to understand that a driver needs a complete package of skills in order to succeed.

Derek interviews Dario Franchetti after he won his third Indy 500. Dario is a detail-oriented choleric.

Ayrton Senna had the complete package and he was driven to be the very best.

Ayrton Senna had an ability to focus intensely on his job.

Ayrton Senna scored an emotional Grand Prix win in Brazil in 1993.

Part of Ayrton Senna's communication style was to shake hands with each of his mechanics each day; they loved it.

Alain Prost's preparation was meticulous, and many believe this gave him an edge.

Prost was another deep thinker who could strategically plan a race and then execute the plan.

Part of Prost's greatness was his ability to be mechanically sympathetic with the car. He won his fourth world championship in a superior car that he helped develop.

Rick Mears won the Indy 500 four times because he was a good feel-sensitive driver and had good mental skills.

LAT

Mario put a lot of thought into the setup of his cars.

Dan Boyd

Dan Boyd

Mario was viewed as a fierce competitor who would make life as difficult as possible for everyone he raced against.

Michael Andretti grew up to be one of the very best racers of his time.

The McLaren team determined that Michael Andretti had not made a total commitment to the team.

Nigel Mansell—shown in Hungary 1986—drained himself mentally and emotionally in a race car.

Nigel Mansell had great mental skills and loved to prove the doubters wrong by winning.

Derek (and others) believe that Michael Schumacher had the strongest desire and commitment of any modern driver. Prior to Ferrari, Schumacher raced on the Benetton team.

Michael Schumacher's commitment to win led him to literally assault drivers with his car, as when he hit Jacques Villeneuve in 1997.

Michael Schumacher had a thorough understanding of the technical side of race cars and had the ability to pull out the magic lap when needed, particularly in Monaco, a race he won five times.

Will Power asks questions relentlessly. Tim Cindric, team manager at Team Penske, says Power is the most prepared driver he has ever worked with.

Helio's fun-loving temperament endears him to sponsors and television cameras.

Helio displays his sanguine temperament for all to see—some teams read this the wrong way with young drivers in that they think they are not serious enough.

Jimmie Johnson has a close and trusting relationship with crew chief Chad Knaus. Together they form a powerhouse combination.

Hamilton's emotional state often dictated the result.

Hamilton was never regarded as being technically accurate and even admitted it when paired with Button at McLaren.

LAT

LAT

LAT

During Jimmie Johnson's pit stops he can order specific changes that keep making his car faster relative to the changing conditions.

Alonso can take slow cars to the podium because of his mistake-free commitment to grab every little opportunity.

Montoya's built-in restrictor is that he is a pure instinct/reflex driver who cannot order the right car setup changes during races.

Alonso prides himself on being a true team leader.

Jeff Gordon is a complete champion.

Dario's choleric temperament drives him to meticulous preparation where the small details can count.

Dario is technically accurate with his feedback and can therefore keep his cars at or near the front because he rarely drives a less-than-perfect car.

Vettel's podiums come because he is the complete package—
perhaps the youngest ever complete package.

Vettel is a choleric temperament who is demanding and relentless. His
sanguine blend allows him to also be light-hearted and fun-loving.

expense, saying Grand Prix drivers don't know what hard work is and most spend their time relaxing in armchairs. Everybody laughed at the time, but for some reason, I did not let it roll off me as I should have.

I had a pretty good qualifying session and the Irish hospitality was in full force in the paddock. I spent the night before the race with family and friends and there was an air of great anticipation when we talked about what might be in the race.

Race day dawned and the buildup only heightened everybody's anticipation of what might come as the afternoon unfolded. I felt good. The car was giving me the right feelings. I had an unusual confidence in the car that day and I eagerly awaited the start.

The start of a Formula 1 race is without doubt the most dangerous time in motorsport. When the green flag flies, the cars all scream away from a standstill with drivers fighting to get the best traction from the rear tires. The run to the first corner usually has drivers' heart rates above 185 beats per minute because of a great adrenalin rush and maybe because of fear.

On the first lap of the race my gearshift came loose and I could not change gears. I had to make an immediate pit stop. The opportunity for glory (a relative term) had disappeared. I was helpless and alone. The all-important machine had broken and so had the hearts of my family and supporters. I was absolutely livid that all the efforts to try to gain a good result had just been thrown away. Ray had made a small mistake and forgot to tighten up the retaining nut on the gearshift after it was adjusted in the cockpit just before the start of the race. By the time he grabbed his wrench and tightened it, I was already in last place and more than half a lap behind.

Almost unbelievably, when I did start to lap at full speed, the car was really fast. I began to catch and pass many cars. Although my efforts were somewhat futile, I still felt compelled to prove a point. Although the race was almost two hours long, it seemed to go by in a flash. The last car I passed before the checkered flag was Jacque Lafitte in the Ligier, who actually finished on the rostrum in third place. It was one of those days where I was on top of my form and the car was very good, and as I closed in on Lafitte I could still feel my anger, because I knew I had missed out on a possible rostrum position in my home Grand Prix. What a day that would have been for me and my friends and family.

At the end of the race, as I walked down the pit road with helmet in hand, I saw Ray walking toward me to offer his congratulations for a job well done. As we approached each other in the pit lane, I was seconds from exhibiting the very poor communication skills I possessed. The first thing that blurted out of my mouth was, "Remember that armchair you mentioned yesterday? Well you must have been sitting in it!"

Ray's face changed immediately. He didn't know whether to respond verbally or physically. A caustic cloud descended over the team. My team manager, John McDonald, sided with Ray and warned me against attacking his employees.

I slowly began to realize my short-term satisfaction gained by blasting Ray might not have been a very professional way to handle things. Little did I know what I did for the morale of the team. I learned in the coming weeks my unwarranted blurt of anger had broken the bond between driver and team. My short-term satisfaction had long-term implications. For the rest of the season we just went through the motions. Ray felt betrayed and, indeed, abused.

If only someone had told me about the art of communication, I could have handled the situation entirely differently and I would have benefited in the long term from a closely knit team.

More than thirty years later, I still remember that outburst and I'm fairly sure Ray also remembers it. You can clearly see I destroyed the vital foundation necessary for harmony within a team, and make no mistake about it, harmony brings speed. Just imagine what might have happened if I had offered my hand to Ray and thanked him for his countless hours of toil and effort, and told him not to worry about the small mistake. I daresay he would have been energized to provide me with the best possible car he could produce for me for the rest of the season.

A CHAMPION'S WAY TO COMMUNICATE

Michael Schumacher was a strong communicator during his career. He was not necessarily a warm personality, but his enormous success endeared him to his hard-working team. He was particularly gifted at communicating with his engineers about what he needed in the car to make him go faster. He was forever curious, always asking questions and always thinking of how to make the car go faster. In this business, if the car does not go fast, there is nothing else that prompts conversation. History has shown he is usually right in the direction he sent the team.

His "thank you" language came in the form of gifts for his mechanics and their families. He commanded a certain respect and his on-track performance energized the teams he was involved with. A great example of this was when Michael drove for the Benetton team between 1992 and 1995. He raised the level of that team to the point where he won two world championships with them. At that same time the Ferrari team couldn't get out of their own way. When Michael left Benetton, the team immediately fell to pieces, and when he joined Ferrari he helped build that team to be the best in the world. If Michael was not as effective a communicator as he was, I daresay the Ferrari team would not have been as successful.

As you ponder about what type of personality you have and how you believe you interact with other people, I would offer a guideline that says rather than look to build friendships with people, look to build respect. Respecting others is a great foundation for them respecting you. Respect in turn builds your friendships. Perhaps the most powerful form of communication from a driver or any leader to a team is to say, "Thank you."

FIVE

MENTAL SKILLS

"Never allow circumstances to dictate your behavior."

I WILL TELL YOU CATEGORICALLY that strong mental skills are the most crucial part of a driver's overall package. Without complete emotional and mental control, it is doubtful you can consistently withstand the enormous pressures at the top of the motorsports mountain, and consequently you cannot consistently produce your peak performance. Try to engrain it in your brain: "What the mind perceives, the body achieves."

Weak mental skills will be your built-in restrictor. This restrictor will always surface when under pressure and trip you up. Strong mental skills are the great separator, the great differentiator, the true difference maker.

In Formula 1 there is tremendous pressure on drivers to perform. Ferrari's Felipe Massa had to endure a mental bombardment after his accident in Hungary in 2010 when the world's press hounded his team to get rid of him. Can you imagine being able to ignore every motorsports specialist magazine and Italian newspaper calling for you to be thrown out of the team?

In the 2010 Formula 1 title race Vettel and Webber knew they were in the fastest cars. Mark Hughes wrote before the Japanese Grand Prix in Suzuka that they each knew they would have to beat each other. Then he wrote, "Gaining and maintaining the psychological upper hand could be the decider here, and from two guys that have yet to win a title that's a fascinating prospect." These are two world-class athletes going head to head in the same machinery and the world media are saying that their mental skills might be the deciding factor—and it was. As it unfolded Webber made mistakes, Vettel made it happen and he became world champion for the first time.

Vettel told *Autosport*'s Edd Straw, "You must learn how to switch off and focus on what really matters—and the only thing that matters to me is to fight for and to win the title." And what got him there was the ability to focus on the process at a higher level than his competition. Being world champion is about being fast, galvanizing the team in your corner and winning the psychological war.

Team owner Frank Williams once said, "If I've learned one thing about racing drivers, it's that the great ones are bastards!"

Three-time Indianapolis 500 winner Dario Franchitti is a driver who is regarded as having great mental strength and preparation, and he's one of racing's greatest thinkers. His calmness in the cockpit and his radio banter during what were some intense on-track battles are frighteningly serene.

Few would doubt Lewis Hamilton is the fastest driver in Formula 1, but Fernando Alonso and Vettel would be regarded as more rounded and complete. If you asked anyone in the paddock in 2011 or 2012 about their opinion of Hamilton as an elite athlete, chances are they would tell you he needs to control the roller coaster that is his head and his emotions. In other words, can you imagine how unbeatable he would be if he had the mental skills of Schumacher, or Alonso?

Autosport's Tony Dodgins wrote in 2012, "Massa displayed the characteristics of a competitor who performs better in an environment in which he is loved and encouraged." Nowhere does that manifest itself better than in his relationship with Rob Smedley, his race engineer since 2006. Together they developed a respect and support system within the Ferrari team. Few would argue that at the time of the accident in Hungary (2009), Ferrari, collectively and emotionally, was Felipe's team.

When he returned from his injuries, perhaps a little insecure about his physical condition, he found Ferrari had fallen in love anew. Alonso had arrived, had his feet well under the table and would prove a formidable adversary. Massa no longer felt the same support, and he began to doubt himself. He was told to "move over" and let Alonso past many times, and he struggled to absorb that type of treatment. Psychologically it was a big blow, and until the end of 2012 when he began to show flashes of his prior brilliance, people doubted he would ever surface again as the rapid performer he once was, all because his environment changed from an emotionally supportive one to a colder, more distant one.

Toward the end of 2012 he summoned just enough performance for Ferrari to give him one more try. "Even if 90 percent of the people do not want to believe in me anymore, it's important you believe in yourself," said Massa. A Ferrari source within the team said, "It was 100 percent about his mental approach, about understanding his role. It was nothing to do with car setup." In other words, the world's press was again given fodder to print around the world the car was fine, it was all in his head. Can you imagine that mental barrage and the skills and strength needed to survive? These might be the skills you may need to compete at the upper echelons of the sport.

The world's greatest athletes, ones who have sustaining power, usually possess great mental strength. Harry Brauvert once wrote in *USA Today* that when Tiger Woods was the world's number-one golfer, his biggest club was his mental strength. He wrote, "His will to win, combined with his physical conditioning, is unrivaled on PGA Tour. For all the physical skills the golf gods gave Tiger Woods, the mental toughness he brings to his sport might be just as important in setting him apart. A fiery competitor who often pumps his fist to punctuate clutch shots, Woods can focus to the exclusion of all else under pressure, especially when a major championship is on the line. He had won eight majors by the age of 28."

Mark O'Meara, probably Woods' closest friend on the tour, says Woods has a single-minded mental toughness that drives him to be the best at whatever he does. Yet he watched that rock crumble in 2009 in one of the sporting world's greatest examples of misplaced thoughts derailing an elite athlete.

To unequivocally prove the point about mental strength having the ability to ultimately control the outcome of competition, consider what happened in 2009 when Woods was embroiled in a personal scandal that rocked his professional and family life, and publically humiliated him on a global stage.

As the scandal played out publically, he took a self-imposed break from golf competition, and since he returned he has not played at the same level again. During his time of exile Woods also went through a knee injury and was dropped by some of the biggest sponsors in the world. Yes, he went through the ringer of chaos in a short space of time, but there is no way his superior physical skills eroded that quickly to produce such a drop in performance upon his return to competition. It was his mental muscle that became somewhat weak and porous.

The turmoil ultimately broke him down. For maybe the first time in his competitive life, doubt crept into his psyche. He was injured just like Massa and he was expected to recover in front of the eyes of the world. He looked more tired, and his trademark drive for perfection was missing. The weight of the absurd expectations that had been placed on him as the former world's number-one golfer was wearing him thin. He was feeling the pressure, and how could he not? The pressure of the scandal had seared the mental muscle. The muscle was injured and he could not repair it in time. It was now weaker and more vulnerable, and it showed in his performance. When the mental muscle looses its shine, so do the results.

I believe that there are racing drivers with this same mindset as the "original" Tiger Woods and remember, the consequences of a Tiger's mistake might mean he loses his ball, but a mistake by a race car driver might mean he loses his life.

Golf's new hero in 2012 was an Irishman, Rory McIlroy. He was about to dominate the Masters with a four-stroke lead going into the final nine holes. Then his game collapsed. He made mistake after mistake and collapsed in front of the eyes of the world. He had failed to convert like a true champion, and the world watched and judged.

USA Today's Steve DiMeglio wrote, "Was the collapse horrifying? Yes. Would it be haunting? Absolutely not. McIlroy insisted that as ugly as his final-round, back-nine Masters collapse was, it would not leave any lasting scars. 'I don't think I was ready,' he said. 'I hit the ball really well that week, the best probably I've ever hit it. It was more mental than anything else, just trying to handle the situation better. Not rushing. Hopefully I'll deal with it better the next time that I'm in one of those situations. I displayed a few weaknesses in my game that I need to work on.'"

Greg Norman also helped him because he had experience being in the same difficult situation where his abilities were questioned around the world. In the 1996 Masters he blew a six-shot lead. He told McIlroy to ignore the media. Don't read magazines or watch the Golf Channel. In other words put up your barrier and protect yourself. McIlroy did use the experience to further develop his mental muscle and become even stronger. He went on to become the number-one ranked golfer in the world. The world's elite athletes have the great ability to forget their mistakes and move on undaunted.

If I looked back at my biggest weakness while I competed in Formula 1 and Indy Cars, it was that I was not as mentally strong as I needed to be to manage outside distractions and therefore sustain great performances. I made too many mistakes under pressure. This led to me throwing away good results in the closing stages of races.

In 1978 at the Austrian Grand Prix, I was presented with an ideal opportunity to shine. It was raining on race day and rain can be a great equalizer. I reveled in the conditions throughout the race, and in the closing stages had brought the low-budget Ensign to fourth place. As the racing line dried, it became more crucial where you placed the car on the road. With 11 laps to go, I made a small mistake and threw it all away with a spin into a wheat field. In one split-second loss of focus, all the hours of effort by my mechanics and all the hopes and dreams of the team slid off the road. My first world championship points were thrown away, and therefore the valuable financial aid the team would have received the following year also disappeared. If only I had maintained my concentration and focus a little longer.

In 1982 while driving for the great Williams Grand Prix team at the Belgian Grand Prix in Zolder, I was running in fifth when Eddie Cheever began to catch me in the Ligier. Instead of concentrating on my own race, I began to get distracted by Cheever and I braked a few feet too late into the first corner. The car locked its rear brakes and I slid off the circuit backward into the fence. Again I had exhibited poor mental skills and made a costly mistake.

In 1983 while driving Indy Cars for Tony Bettenhausen at Road America, I was running in third with a handful of laps to go when I made a small mistake going through the 160-mph kink. I slipped off the road and crashed.

These three incidents highlight what my main weakness was and how I practiced the genesis of self-sabotage. If only I had learned how to have better mental skills and therefore better control of the outcome. How much more valuable might I have been to a team if I did not make those silly errors of judgment? If someone had alerted me to my weakness, would I have accepted it or run from it? Although it goes against the grain of most drivers, admitting and identifying a weakness is 90 percent of the way to curing it.

Data is a great telltale for driver performance, particularly a driver's consistency. In qualifying, for example, the data readouts will show a driver's fastest lap and will have it broken down into multiple timed sectors. The data will then be able to add together a driver's theoretical fastest lap possible if he was able to add all of his fastest sectors no matter when in a particular run they occurred. The closer the actual fastest lap is to the theoretical fastest lap, the more perfect the driver was on that lap. A driver only becomes perfect when he is mistake-free and accurately hitting all of the right reference points. Mistake-free laps (or close to) while hitting the right reference points are the very foundation of consistently. And strong mental skills will give a driver the ability to focus and put together mistake-free performances when under extreme pressure.

Will Power has proven to have an innate ability to put together consistent, mistake-free laps that have his actual lap time very close to his theoretical fastest more often than most drivers. For him this is a strength, and many drivers would like to have or be able to develop that same strength, and it is almost invaluable to a team.

Identifying all weaknesses will put you on the road to success if you are committed to being the very best you can be.

OTHER STARS

I always find it fascinating to compare the mental makeup of great drivers. Kimi Raikkonen and Juan Montoya are regularly compared. In November 2004, English journalist Nigel Roebuck did an accurate comparison that read like this:

"Raikkonen rarely betrays more than a withering glance of emotion, doesn't let in anything that's not relevant to the job in hand. Montoya, fiery and extroverted, wears his heart on his sleeve, and the styles of their racing reflect these traits. Kimi's performances are relentless; Juan Pablo's are a heady mix of adrenaline and opportunism. Raikkonen retains his icy calm every second he's in the car; Montoya uses emotion to drive his performances. Each trait has its upsides and downsides.

"Raikkonen has the dimmer switch on the outside world turned way down and there are no distractions.

"Raikkonen's personality lends itself better to focus, Montoya's is perfect for the element of ambush that wins him races.

"Both drivers are generally immune to pressure from behind, more so than Michael Schumacher. No quarter is given, though each is scrupulously fair in battle, with very fine judgment.

"Montoya will be good at the well-timed wind-up. Just as Kimi will be good in not even acknowledging it.

"The team can perhaps help him in finding more consistent technical solutions than he was able to do at Williams.

"Kimi is just as fast, more flexible, calmer, and already has the momentum of a good team relationship. Nothing is going to faze him, not even a sister silver car going around his outside in a place he'd never even considered."

Make no mistake about it, both Montoya and Raikkonen have exhibited these same mental and emotional traits since they were small boys.

MENTAL PRESSURE. DO YOU FEEL IT OR APPLY IT?

Motor racing makes very high demands on us mentally. We are expected to perform in a dangerous sport under enormous pressure with the eyes of the world firmly focused on us. No matter how critical of us our peers are, or how caustic the media is, you must not let your guard down for several reasons. Firstly, mistakes can kill you in a race car, and secondly, at all times, there will be any number of drivers ready and waiting to step into our seat at the slightest opportunity. What other sport do you know where a player can be killed, and there would be a line of willing players ready to step into his place? Motorsport is a colorful, glamorous sport that can be so savage and brutal. It is your job to always rise above this.

There will always be pressure when competing at a world-class level in anything, but if you allow the pressure to disrupt your routine and decision making you are a driver who feels the pressure. If you use the situations to your advantage and destabilize your opposition, you are a driver who applies the pressure. Try to make sure you are the applier.

Every young driver has a unique mental makeup. While it is a given that everyone needs emotional support of some sort, some drivers require vastly different types of support.

If we talk mental strength, we are talking about what takes place in the head. Whenever there is talk of what goes on inside the head, I have found that most young drivers run for cover. That's because most young drivers will try to hide a weakness, particularly if it has to do with the head. The head is also one of the most complex areas to work with. There is no doubt that working with any world-class athlete can be a real challenge.

Picture your mental capacity as being like a power generator. If your generator has a capacity of 20,000 watts, and during a hot and difficult race you start to need 25,000 watts, your "lights" will start to dim, and the capacity needed to power any new requirements is just not there. This will lead to the fuse blowing and everything will be shut down. When this happens, a race car is probably flying off the road backward.

The key for any competitive race car driver is to have at least enough capacity in your personal generator to be competitive. The champions usually have excess capacity, because that allows them to be able to process more inputs when necessary without going into overload.

If you are not physically strong enough to compete at the most difficult time of a race, you will begin to draw upon the mental capacity "power generator" for support. If there is no spare capacity, the car starts to get ahead of the driver, as opposed to the other way around. When the race car is ahead of the driver, the driver no longer controls his environment. His environment is being controlled by his circumstances (too tired, too hot, mentally drained), and that is the danger zone for a driver.

If you are a superb, physically prepared athlete, and not particularly physically challenged in the race car during a hot and difficult event, you will have that spare mental capacity available to be used for other challenges. These might be for race strategy, or thinking how to position yourself for the best possible chance to win, or logging crucial setup/performance information you can then mentally download to your race engineers for them to use for performance enhancements in later events. The champions have great mental capacity and always have the ability to stay ahead of the race car. Champions who have exhibited great mental capacity during races are Fernando Alonso, Michael Schumacher and Indy 500 winners Dan Wheldon and Rick Mears.

MENTALLY TOUGH

Formula 1 world champion Nigel Mansell is a superb example of a driver with so much belief in himself that he needed very little emotional support from a team. During his competitive career, no matter what happened, he was able to brush it off and move on to the next level. Nigel was my teammate in the European Formula 2 championship at Donnington Park in 1978. He failed to even qualify for the race because he just didn't get the equipment he needed to show his skills. This was an example of another blow to his ego that he simply absorbed and moved on.

Few people believed Nigel would ever make it to the big time. However, he proved over and over again he just might be mentally the toughest driver I have ever known.

When he drove for my old team, Williams Grand Prix, he blossomed because he didn't care what they thought of his quirky behavior. All he wanted from them was the best car on the grid, which they gave him, and the rest is history, because he went on to become world champion with a spectacular season in 1992. He did all this in a team that is emotionally cold and that is not known for emotionally supporting its driver.

EMOTIONALLY VULNERABLE

Other very talented Williams Formula 1 drivers did not flourish in the team's emotionally cold atmosphere. German Formula 1 driver Heinz Harold Frentzen (Williams 1997–1998) has always needed far more emotional support than Nigel Mansell ever did. During his time at Williams, Frentzen's true talent became buried under emotional distractions and pressures, and the team doubting his abilities, which resulted in him second-guessing himself. It got so bad he could not perform at his peak, and although he was a winner at Williams, he eventually got fired. When he moved to Jordan Grand Prix, a team who nurtures drivers, Frentzen flourished and went on to have his finest days in Formula 1, winning several Grands Prix and almost winning the world championship in 1999.

Consider the fact that Frentzen and Michael Schumacher came from Germany, and had the same background of karting and Formula 3. They were both signed by Mercedes-Benz for their young driver development program, and they both drove the Mercedes Group C car in the World Sports Car championship. There was a time when some people believed Frentzen was actually faster than Schumacher. However, when they both made it to Formula 1, Schumacher's superior mental skills and high levels of ultimate preparation left Frentzen in the dust. Schumacher had no interest in other drivers, in their speed or in their overall performance. He had total confidence in his own abilities, and focused every moment working at improving himself, his car and his teams. The intense pressure of Formula 1 was easy to absorb for Schumacher.

Frentzen, on the other hand, enjoyed himself driving for the Sauber Formula 1 team and developed well. Sauber is well known for its friendly and supportive atmosphere. The pressure increased immensely when Frentzen went to drive for Williams Formula 1. The pressure proved to be too much and his progress stopped. In fact, his career almost ended until it was rescued by Jordan Grand Prix.

A potential big star who never flourished because of weak mental skills was Heikki Kovalainen. I believe it is accurate to say Kovalainen was ill-equipped mentally when he arrived in Formula 1. The pressure of Formula 1 stifled his ability to perform at the highest levels. In an interview with Adam Cooper in 2007, he said, "It's quite clear that when I was in the previous two teams [McLaren and Renault] I didn't get the best out of the car, and I didn't get the best out of the team most of the time, for various reasons [Read: poor mental strength skills]. And I think consequently your self-confidence is going down, you're not feeling as comfortable. I lost the touch for a while—it's like a golfer loses his swing. I had to take a step back and start again."

While in the lower formula the pressure was much less for him, and he showed his great ability. After he was spat out by the two high-pressure teams (McLaren and Renault), he moved to the much-lower-expectation, low-pressure environment of the new Caterham team and he again flourished. "I drove much better in my junior formula years," Kovalainen said, "then it all sort of started to go in the wrong direction for various reasons, which I don't want to talk too much about." He doesn't have to tell us, we already know what his weakness was and how it became his inbuilt restrictor.

Do you know what type of emotional support you like? What type of emotional environment did you thrive in as a child? What were your emotional and mental hot buttons? Were you a family supported type of individual? Did you perform well when your family was there to support you? Did you perform better when you were away from your immediate family? This type of question will lead you in the direction of what type of mental environment you will thrive in.

Do you think race teams know and understand what type of emotional support a driver needs? Frankly, it has been my experience most teams have no idea about mental and emotional environments.

Do you know how to get yourself into the environment you need to be in to flourish? How strong mentally do you think you are? Can you withstand the distractions of life and always perform at your peak level of performance?

Always remember: You are what you believe. Your behavior is always a byproduct of your belief system.

When distracted or emotionally disturbed, you can be transferred from that state by the renewing of your mind. In other words you need to think differently. You need to think good, positive things about yourself. Lasting change occurs in the mind first. Great drivers can always renew their minds and become the drivers they believe they are.

Circumstances dictate the mental state of many drivers, but unfortunately circumstances are always subject to change. Circumstances also dictate your emotions, and circumstances are always in a state of flux.

Your belief system needs to be based on truth, not on circumstances. However, if you do not act on what you believe, which is hopefully the truth, you flounder and continue to be dictated by your circumstances and therefore by your emotional state.

Heinz Harald Frentzen was a reactive driver who had weak mental skills and behaved according to his circumstances. As his circumstances changed, so did his behavior, and therefore he was always in a state of change and unstable. His speed and ability was unchanged, but his ability to access that speed and ability consistently was a little fuzzy.

Overly reactive people are constantly being driven by their insecurities and fears. Schumacher, on the other hand, was not dictated by his circumstance. He was dictated by his belief system. You are what you think; Michael Schumacher is what he thinks, Frentzen and Massa are also what they think.

Respected journalist Mark Hughes also had an interesting take on mental strength.

He believed that although all competitive sports require a certain mental pitch to be achieved, he considered motorsports as being at the extreme end of the scale, saying, "It's more complex than most sports and more dangerous. As well as the concern about achieving your own maximum competitive performance, there's the whole complex matrix of the car to consider, all against a subconscious backdrop of self-preservation.

"Uncertainty is the enemy of getting in the zone. That and emotion, but emotion's a strange one, a dangerous force in that it can be used to tease out depths of performance, but can just as easily turn on you.

"I've always felt that the way for someone to beat Michael would be to create doubt in his mind.

"Michael's incredibly mentally strong and that was shown clearly in 1996 when he had a dog of a car, but still won races. It's so easy in that situation to get yourself into a spiral of negativity that affects your performance."

Nigel Mansell was one of the most exciting and aggressive drivers F1 has ever seen, yet he did not need big doses of emotional support from the team. For him it was almost as if the performances were rooted in proving everyone wrong. Unusually, Mansell seemed to use his paranoia in a positive way.

Senna had the persona of a warrior. He seemed to thrive in a war zone. Senna, in fact, was one of the very few who took that dangerous partner, emotion, and danced with it. Tragically, it probably killed him, just as it did Gilles Villeneuve.

Three-time Formula 1 world champion Jackie Stewart used to describe how he would try to "deflate like a balloon" before he got in the car, to drain himself of all emotion, so he could operate with coldly clinical precision.

Finns Mika Hakkinen and Kimi Raikkonen seem to be utterly devoid of emotion anywhere near a car.

It's clear when looking at this subject that there are as many different types of mental strength as there are drivers. It's also apparent that traits that are strengths in certain situations are flaws in others. Where there's no room for doubt, how do you rationalize defeat? How do you find room to improve? But when you acknowledge the scope to get better, how do you prevent awkward questions creeping in about the strengths of others? How do you prevent yourself conspiring to let them defeat you? Questions, always questions. The really tough guys answer them, then forget them. The others hold them at bay.

1978 Formula 1 World Champion Mario Andretti is a man who has seen it all. His words are well respected. He was once quoted as saying, "Not too many people know how to win. A lot of people know how to go fast and they'll be a factor, but knowing how to win is knowing how to control your emotions. I see drivers who are quick, they'll be up front for a while, but you know they'll never win. They'll make a mistake; they'll do something that will cause them not to be there in the end. They just don't have the capacity, the capability, to have that mental strength."

Like him or not, a driver who has consistently displayed great mental strength is Ireland's Eddie Irvine. Throughout his early career, Eddie had such a belief in himself that his attitude toward his profession was almost arrogant. As he prepared to enter Formula 1 in 1992, a time in most drivers' lives that is the realization of their dream, he treated the event almost with distain. He was part of a famous incident in the Japanese Grand Prix when the great Ayrton Senna was trying to lap him, and Eddie had no interest in showing any level of respect. As a result, Senna sought him out after the race to scold him. Irvine's arrogant attitude to the world champion resulted in a fistfight.

For the next 10 years of Irvine's Formula 1 career while driving for teams such as Jordan, Jaguar and Ferrari, he continued to show the same level of arrogance, but, more importantly, he was never mentally distracted by other drivers or his circumstances. Irvine provoked people by his comments and actions, but he never allowed himself to be provoked. He used his words to distract his opposition, but their response, no matter how acrid, was never allowed to penetrate his mental moat. People loved or hated Irvine, but he never cared one way or the other.

2010 Formula 1 World Champion Jenson Button is a great example of a driver who appears to have strong mental skills. After just one season in the British Formula 3 championship, he was thrown straight into Formula 1 with the Williams Team. The car suited his style and he had a superb rookie season. Because Williams already had Juan Montoya under contract, they had to loan out Button to the Renault Team for his second season.

The Renault was nowhere near as good a car and Button struggled all season long. The team manager for Renault, the flamboyant Flavio Briatore, began to publicly criticize Button and actually said if he did not improve during the 2002 season, he would be out of F1. Button had also drawn public criticism from many sides about his lavish spending and his playboy lifestyle.

With this type of scrutiny and public criticism, in addition to the intense pressure of Formula 1, Button could have easily buckled under the pressure. However, as all elite athletes do, his personal belief system allowed him to block out all the distractions and he had a great 2002 season. His most important test was not whether he could sort out a race car or whether he could drive it fast, it was whether he could mentally succeed in the fish tank with the piranhas of Formula 1. He had used his 2002 season to display again all his talents and skills in front of a critical media and interested team owners. After surviving the test, and proving his strong mental skills by withstanding that type of pressure, Button has assured himself of his place in Formula 1.

Then to prove his point again, he had to draw upon all of his mental skills during his championship run with Brawn F1. Much was written about Button by the British media regarding his title chances that depended on his mental preparation for the last five races amid fears that he was choking under the pressure of leading the world championship. The fear was he was beginning to concentrate on the prize and not the process. Or as some psychologists will say, he was becoming *outcome* focused and not *process* focused.

In what was an open media discussion in England, it was stated that once you've won six out of seven races as Button did at the start of the season, that it would be easy to switch your focus onto the outcome, that of actually winning the world championship. That's when a fear of failure can come in. Early in the season, Button was very process focused and kept saying he wasn't thinking about the championship. The fear in England was that he was finding it tough to stay process focused. When an athlete struggles to maintain this one-at-a-time process mentality, it can send him into a downward spiral.

The message was clear for Button. His destiny was in his own hands and in the strength of his mental skills. He dug deep, kept outside distractions to a minimum and became world champion. Many believe that performance developed his skills to an even higher level, and when he went up against Lewis Hamilton at McClaren, he was equipped and ready.

One of the relative newcomers against Button during the 2003 season was Finland's Kimi Raikkonen. At the time Raikkonen was one of the most unusual drivers to appear on the scene for many years. He appears to be emotionally cold and unaffected by his surroundings. He is affection-ately called the Ice Man. Amazingly when he reached the top by winning a Grand Prix, he stunned many by consid-ering the win to be no big deal.

A story in *Formula One* magazine at the end of the 2003 again highlighted the Ice Man when he was asked what winning that first Grand Prix really meant. "Nothing, really," came the flippant response. "I guess it makes you know you can win, that's the only thing. It doesn't make you half-a-second quicker, just a bit more confident. Maybe you know you can win races when you have a good package and a good day, but that's about it."

This response shocked most people who have blood running through their veins. It certainly shocked all Rubens Barrichello fans when they thought back to Barrichello's first Grand Prix win in Germany when he openly wept on the victory podium. These are two very different drivers and one is not necessarily right or wrong, but Raikkonen certainly shows the emotional coldness that has shown itself to be somewhat of an advantage when under severe pressure.

Whatever driver one might profile as an example of what to do or not to do, there is always one standout in the "admire" column and that is again Michael Schumacher. Regarding his mental strength, one of his great attributes is that he never allows himself to become discouraged or depressed.

Whenever Schumacher is compared to the great Ayrton Senna, especially in the area of mental strength, Formula 1 team owner Frank Williams will always tell you Senna "had astonishing mental preparation."

All of these real life stories simply prove some drivers can and some drivers can't overcome the mental distractions of motorsports at the top level. Those who can, possess a special and necessary skill. If that skill is not already engrained within your mental makeup, you can learn that skill. You can learn it by first recognizing what it is and then starting to renew your mind. My wife Rhonda's favorite saying is "renewing of the mind" and it is a powerful step forward for everybody no matter what they do in life.

You can do the very same by believing in yourself. Do not let distractions affect your performance. Move away from distractions that affect your performance. Surround yourself with positive and supportive people. Because life in general has many distractions, develop the habit and skill of renewing your mind. It will clear the road for you to display all of your natural talents every time you step into competition. Just look around you and you can tell who makes the mistakes and who does not. Make sure you are the one who is considered the solid one. You are what you believe about yourself.

HOW TO DEVELOP THE MENTAL STRENGTH OF A CHAMPION

Before we get into this subject, please don't fear the admission you might need help in this area. If you do, believe me, the quicker you admit you could benefit from strengthening your mental muscle, the quicker you will become more effective in a race car.

What if a lack of mental strength is a weakness that needs to be boosted in a driver, just like it was with me? Where would you go, what might you do? The first thing to do is to be quietly honest with yourself, and admit it is an area you would like to strengthen. Then I would seek help from a professional.

There are many sports psychologists who work with athletes; however, I believe you need to choose someone who has a firm understanding of the requirements of motorsports. Performance specialist Dr. Jacques Dallaire of Performance Prime (www.performanceprime.com) is one of those people who has dedicated a large portion of his life to developing race car drivers. I have a personal connection with Performance Prime because I was one of their early studies when the late Dr. Dan Marisi was an active partner. In fact, I still carry my personal "act model" card in my wallet that was created for me by Dan before he died.

Performance Prime applies principles of sport science technology to the development and delivery of products and services designed to improve individual and group or team performance. This is the core business that serves as the engine for the Performance Prime Development Initiative, as much as a laboratory for product development. The company's development strategy leverages the unique capabilities, experience, reputation and client base of Performance Prime (developed over the past 20 years) to produce products based on sports science technology that flow from their core program, and make them available to identifiable segments of the larger population. This includes sport participants at all levels and in all sports, the medical and rehabilitation community, the education community, the occupational and business community, older adults and children.

In 1983, two scientists from Canada embarked on a mission to improve the performance of motorsport athletes and other high performers. As the programs have evolved, so have the number and variety of professionals who have sought out the assistance of Performance Prime specialists to improve their performance. To date, Performance Prime has worked with clients in virtually every form of motorsport, a broad selection of individual and team sports, law enforcement, surgeons, pilots, firefighters, sales professionals, corporate executives and, most recently, air-traffic controllers. The mental skills in particular that underlie championship performance are common to all of these endeavors and this accounts for the diversity of the HPI clientele.

Virtually all high-performance people acknowledge that 80 percent of the game is mental, and it doesn't matter whether we are talking about a professional golfer, an Olympic athlete, a SWAT team specialist, a company CEO or a top salesman. They recognize it is not their physical prowess or their knowledge that ensures success in the competitive world in which they live and work, but rather their personal success is most influenced by the mental skills they are able to bring to bear. They have come to recognize the brain is like a muscle. It is the most powerful weapon in your arsenal, and you need to exercise it and train it in order to achieve and maintain peak performance.

Dr. Dallaire's book, *Performance Thinking*, is a valuable learning component that can be used by drivers to understand at a higher level what some believe to be the intangible of mental skills.

HABITUAL BEHAVIOR PATTERNS

In order to function as human beings, we rely on habitual behavior patterns. We are all creatures of habit and our habits shape our future. Elite athletes do not decide their future, they decide their habits and their habits decide their future. What are your habits? Who is monitoring what you do?

Complex skills such as managing teams, selling and strategic leadership are made up of more basic human skills such as communicating, decision making, organizing, delegating and so on. Just like the complex skill of driving a race car is made up of knowledge, planning, communication, decision making, execution and physical control skills, which when assembled together enable you to drive a race car on its limit at high speed and safely while processing many other things at the same time. It is a learned pattern of automatic or unconscious behavior that eventually becomes your habit.

So how do you ensure your habits are correct? This is where you may want to add a coach. A coach (I like to refer to them as components) can help you discover where your skills are optimal, and where there are behavior patterns that are limiting your performance.

If you decide a personal coach is for you, there are some basic steps you will have to go through. The first step is to make sure the coach has been to the top of the mountain you want to climb. The second step is to establish a goal for yourself at the outcome of the coaching (you will never hit a target you never set). This will enable you to measure your own performance, and that of your coach, against a specific achievable objective. As long as you are positively and congruently motivated toward that goal, you will be almost guaranteed to achieve an excellent result.

The final step is to develop new strategies that will enable you to achieve a level of performance and consistently deliver the results you want. Your coach will work with you as you implement these new behavior patterns, enabling you to explore the exciting new opportunities that will open up for you.

Motorsports is one of the most complex sports in the world, with very little complex coaching support. Parents often make the mistake of thinking that because they were successful at business they could apply the same principles to their motorsports activities. This has proven to be an expensive mistake many times in the past. If your son was primed for a career in the NFL, why would you think you would know more about how to develop him than a team's specialized coaches? Yet it happens on a daily basis in motorsports—a complex sport that very few parents understand.

SIX

PHYSICAL FITNESS

*When the doctors reviewed the results, they
were shocked. I had the highest sustained heartbeat
of any athlete they had ever measured during
competition at that time.*

BEFORE YOU READ a word of this, I want you to know I have never studied physical fitness in detail and have no qualifications to tell you what to do or not do. I can only offer you examples of what I personally lived through as a professional athlete, and what I have seen others live through in the physically demanding world of motor-sports. There are lots of professional trainers available that specialize in motorsports training, so expert advice is available.

Although races early in a career are relatively short events, they still require a certain level of physical fitness, which provides a foundation for the future when you might be driving heavy cars for two or three hours, or for what might be expected of you during an endurance race such as the Le Mans 24 Hours. Being race-fit in the lower formulae is relatively easy when the races are 12 or 15 laps. However, what about when you go testing and have to run 100 laps? This is where you need to be physically fit enough to offer accurate and relevant information.

Roger Penske once told me all the small details make the big things possible. I could not agree more because of the specialized arena we now operate in. Jenson Button says, "It's not just about driving fast. It can even be about nutrition, about being more alert. Some drivers take pills to help them see in the dark for certain races like Monaco so that their eyes immediately work with the light in the tunnel, and they brake for the chicane with vision at 100 percent. There are so many competitive drivers who you are always looking for something else." Physical fitness is part of that something else.

Many people just see a driver behind the wheel and have no idea that a considerable physical effort must be put forth to achieve optimum performance from the vehicle. I have personally experienced everything physically in a race car. I have finished Grand Prix races fresh and alert, and I have also collapsed from exhaustion. I have dealt with all sorts of pain, particularly cramps, and during a particularly difficult time in my career when I suffered physical difficulties on a regular basis, I had reason to question my own training routine. Through it all I learned the basics about physical readiness to drive race cars.

Physical fitness and how to achieve it is unique to each individual. Each person's metabolism works in a unique way, and it is very important to recognize what type of metabolism you have. For example, I would always perspire a lot when in a race car; therefore I needed a lot of liquid replenishment loaded with minerals. Other drivers such as five-time Formula 1 world champion Michael Schumacher never look sweaty or exhausted after a race, and former Williams Formula 1 driver Thierry Boutsen would not even have his hair out of place after a race, whereas I regularly looked pale and sometimes physically wrecked.

I clearly remember during the closing stages of the 1982 U.S. Grand Prix at Caesars Palace in Las Vegas, I was so physically drained with five laps to go that I began to experience dizzy spells under braking.

Immediately after the Spanish Grand Prix in 1980, I was so dehydrated that as soon as I got out of the car I immediately began to gulp down a large bottle of iced water. The shock of the cold water to my dehydrated body caused me to go dizzy and collapse. As I began to fall, I called out to my fellow driver and future teammate Keke Rosberg. I woke up with Keke pounding on my chest in a state of panic, because he thought my heart had stopped. I was taken to the medical center where an IV replenished the fluids and I quickly recovered.

When you replenish, make sure you replenish what your particular body needs. Between fluids and body fat, trainers can have lengthy discussions. Well, what does that mean to a race car driver?

Consider what trainer Mike Collier said regarding the horrid humidity in Sepang, Malaysia, in 2011: "We're looking for the driver to have around 8 percent body fat. You don't really want to go below that here, because you'd be in trouble with dehydration like Alonso was here a couple of years ago when he fainted. We have a different hydration strategy to a standard European race, in terms both of the amount you drink and the composition of the drink.

"The whole point of hydration is a) to replace the nutrients lost to sweat, and b) to increase the volume of blood circulating. In Europe the drink would be electrolyte-based with some carbohydrates, whereas here you want the protein to increase the blood-plasma volume. Typically the driver will lose four to five kg during the race, but with the increased blood volume it's less, maybe three to five kg. There's a lower oxygen content at this humidity. You cannot dissipate the heat, so you don't get evaporation, so you're not able to cool the body, and it increases the demand on the body by 15–20 percent. Jenson Button lost his drink bottle here once and began to lose his vision, a combination of dehydration and the inability to dissipate heat.

"If you can't cool the body then your heart rate starts banging away, and when you add heat and humidity you sweat more and the heart rate increases even more, and the ability to concentrate on things are altered. Some of the simpler natural things—to see and react—are slowed. That's a bad situation in a car doing 200 mph," Collier said.

In 1984, the Hovik Medical Group monitored my heart rate throughout the Long Beach Grand Prix. They were astonished to learn that over the course of the two-hour race I averaged 178 beats per minute with a high of 199. They had never measured an athlete with such sustained high beats before. In fact, they doubted their results initially until similar numbers were later confirmed at another race. Further study at that time showed the only athletes with sustained heart beats as high as race car drivers were professional cyclists. This test caused them to recalibrate their thinking about the physical requirements of driving a race car.

PHYSICAL CONTROL THROUGH THE MIND

During the 1988 Le Mans 24-hour race, I was driving for the biggest team there, Jaguar. I was part of a five-car assault and a multi-million-dollar attack to try to win the most prestigious endurance race in the world. Our car finished fourth with our sister car winning. During the race, I have vivid memories of having severe cramps in my legs and feet and that was at 3 a.m. as I stood in the pit lane with my seat back in hand ready to get in to do a two-hour double stint. That was when I learned how important mind control was. I had to mentally slow my body, without slowing the car. When I mentally slowed my body, the physical exertion was less and I was able to make it through a two-hour stint close enough to the ultimate pace, even though my body's starting point was severely depleted.

REALITY OF THE GYM

Let me tell you the truth about working out to get ready to drive a race car. I don't care how much training you do in the gym, and what level of personal trainer you have, you will not become totally race-fit without being in the race car actually experiencing the activity. You simply cannot replicate the g-forces exerted upon the body while at speed no matter what type of exercise you do. After a long layoff, or when driving a bigger car for the first time, your forearms, wrists and neck still will ache until those body parts raise their tolerance as you get more mileage in that type of car.

You can, however, use the gym to make your body strong enough to be able to adapt more quickly to the rigors of driving a race car.

Why should peak physical conditioning be a requirement? Well, it wasn't as necessary in my day in Formula 1 (1978–1982). Mario Andretti and Niki Lauda never bothered with workouts. Mario would never spend his youth in a gym, and Lauda never looked anything more than an average physical specimen, yet they both won championships.

Today, however, the bar has been raised, initially by Michael Schumacher and now by just about everyone. Have you ever seen Michael Schumacher look physically drained after a race? It's not too long ago three-time Formula 1 world champion Ayrton Senna had to be lifted from his car at the end of a Grand Prix. Another three-time champion, Nelson Piquet, collapsed on the podium after winning his home Grand Prix in Brazil. Their level of physical fitness at that time was just about enough to get the job done, but today it is all very different. Today every discipline from karts to Formula 1 is more competitive. If you have an equal kart as the rest of the field, perhaps your physical conditioning can make the difference between whether you win or are part of the rest of the field. Remember, as you dehydrate, your mental capacity begins to diminish and your opportunity to make mistakes increases.

During the Le Mans 24-hour race with Jaguar in 1988, I discussed my cramping dilemma with the team trainer Tom

Ryan. At that time in my career, as muscle cramping became more of an issue for me, I began to increase my workouts to raise my tolerance level. Tom asked to see my workout routine, and after studying it carefully he simply said that I needed to cut my workouts at least by half. He said I was too tired to drive effectively and my extensive workout routine was not giving my body enough time to rest and rejuvenate. That was a very interesting lesson. I stopped working out for the rest of the season and got stronger, and my mid-race cramping was gone.

Another reason for physical fatigue in a race car is not being relaxed. Instead of treating the steering with a delicate touch, some drivers hang on with a white-knuckle grip that physically taxes their bodies much more. World champion Nigel Mansell would grip the steering wheel of the Williams F1 car tightly and literally manhandle the car to the point where he would be physically and mentally exhausted after a race. When I drove for Jaguar at Le Mans, we had a steering sensor that would document which drivers would physically use more input through the steering to do the same lap time. The high-physical-input drivers would also wear out the steering joints faster than a driver with a delicate touch. Coincidently, the drivers with high physical input through the steering column would also be harder on the brakes and would use more tires and fuel to do the same lap time.

RELAX AND ENJOY

A relaxed driving position with deep breathing and a delicate touch on the steering wheel is much more efficient. Not every driver is naturally inclined to drive this way. However, the more aware you are of this style, the more likely you will be to use it to your advantage. I personally know this works, because I forced myself to drive the Jaguar like this in Le Mans and could do a two-hour stint, at speeds up to 250 mph, on the verge of cramping, but without losing time or positions on the track.

READING YOUR BODY

The lesson here is that tuning for optimum physical fitness is very much like tuning for optimum performance from the race car. Just as the car will tell you what it wants or needs, your body will do exactly the same. It is your job (or with the help of a personal trainer) to read all the messages accurately and act upon the needs as required. If you make mistakes with the setup of the car, you will pay the price. If you make mistakes with your physically conditioning, you will also pay the price.

If you perspire a lot like I did, carefully read the situation and make sure you pre-hydrate and replenish as often as possible with mineral-loaded drinks. Give your body the opportunity to turn your food into useful strength and energy by giving your body good nourishment. Alcohol apparently stays in your blood stream for up to 48 hours, so think about whether you want to compromise your abilities in any way by drinking too much alcohol the night before a race.

Whatever muscle group gets sore while driving, work on those muscles specifically. In 1982 my Formula 1 teammate Keke Rosberg elected not to work out his neck muscles, and instead tied his helmet to both sides to the cockpit, which allowed him to withstand the g-forces of the Williams FW08, and keep his head upright.

Keke won the world championship that year, but that type of casual physical preparation would not suffice today. (Keke was also a smoker and drinker). Whenever you can make the driving position more comfortable or cooler, do it. Most of all, the biggest saving of physical strength is driving in a relaxed and efficient mode. Austria's Niki Lauda, a three-time world champion, had this efficient style, as did Ireland's John Watson (five-time Grand Prix winner). Sometimes you may have to talk yourself into this mode while driving, and talk yourself into the rhythm you need to be energy efficient while you still drive fast.

If you want to be a champion in the mold of a Michael Schumacher or Alonso or Vettel, the bar height has already been set for you. If you can work to having anything close to the physical preparation of these champions, you will have eliminated any physical questions from your artillery. The question is, how do you reach this level?

SPECIALIZED TRAINING

You can go to any reputable gym in any country and find a very good trainer who will put you in the best physical shape of your life. However, because motorsports makes unusual physical demands on the body, if you are aiming for the top you would be better off choosing a trainer who has a more specialized approach to training a race car driver.

One such person is Jim Leo, owner of PitFit Training in Indianapolis. Jim has a wealth of knowledge and experience with race car drivers, and if I was to set myself a specific target, I would like to have someone beside me who could aim me in the right direction. I have included a section penned by Jim himself that accurately sets a driver on the right path as he prepares to endure the physical rigors of racing at high speed.

THE PITFIT APPROACH BY JIM LEO

When most people thought of race car drivers in the past, the vision of a cigarette-smoking, beer-drinking, woman-izing cad usually came to mind. It didn't help this was not too far from the what the public often saw when they went to a race track or tuned into a race on television.

The heroes such as James Hunt in Formula 1, A.J. Foyt in Indy Car, and Tony Stewart in NASCAR emphasized that one could have success on the race track without any type of specialized fitness training. And while this attitude for Formula 1 drivers carried far into the 1990s, a trend that started with the legendary Ayrton Senna and then expanded with Michael Schumacher and others placed a much greater emphasis on improving on-track performance by developing the human performance of the driver. Tony Stewart, however, even at the start of the 2013 season, still stuck to his belief that physical fitness only makes a difference if you somehow have to push the car sometime.

When I started working with Team Penske in 1993, there was little information available to educate a young trainer on what type of training would be most beneficial for a race car driver. My education began with asking drivers where they felt they needed the most focus. But the drivers in CART at the time didn't really seem to think that being fit would make much of an impact on their racing, so I had to keep watching and learning.

When the influx of Formula 1 drivers came in the mid-to-late 1990s, they brought with them the focus on physical fitness and nutrition that was so prevalent in European racing. These drivers had grown up watching Senna and Schumacher train like madmen, then go out and drive with the kind of mastery that personified perfection. Many Formula 1 teams had their own trainers, or physiotherapists, that not only designed customized racing fitness regimes, but also traveled with the drivers to the races to look after them with hydration, nutrition, stretching, massage and injury treatment. When many of these drivers such as Mark Blundell, Gil de Ferran, Alex Zanardi, and Mauricio

Gugelmin arrived to race in CART, they brought this same dedication with them. And once these same drivers started to dominate in CART, even the old-school American drivers such as Bobby Rahal took notice and started training.

Today, fitness training for drivers is the standard at all levels. In Indy Car drivers such as Scott Dixon, Will Power and James Hinchcliffe all place heavy emphasis on their fitness. NASCAR driver Carl Edwards is in such tremendous shape he is regularly featured on the cover of fitness magazines. And in all the series leading up to the highest level, from karting to sprint cars to Indy Lights, drivers make fitness training part of their preseason preparation. You still have the odd driver who looks down at getting into better shape. Tony Stewart obviously isn't a fan of going to the gym and eating healthy, and he still wins in NASCAR. But the question remains how many more championships might he have if he placed more emphasis on his fitness and nutrition.

PHYSIOLOGICAL EFFECTS OF RACING

The specific combined stresses to the human body while driving a race car are unique to the sport and seldom found in any other activity. While certain aspects such as heat stress are commonly found in sports such as triathlon, running and cycling, these athletes are not flying along at speeds often above 150 mph. And while the alert football quarterback has to be continuously aware of the entire field, defense and offense, the average NFL play lasts around five seconds. An Indy 500 participant has to be aware for three hours!

GRAVITATIONAL FORCES

One of the unique stresses a race car driver faces is from gravitational forces, or g-forces. A g-force is essentially a force acting on a body as a result of acceleration or gravity. If a 175-pound driver experiences three g's in a corner, this is equivalent to having 525 pounds of force applied. The driver faces g-forces from all directions, although the most severe are normally lateral g's in a corner and frontal g's upon deceleration under braking. The effects of g-forces on a driver can be minor, such as light difficulty in breathing, or severe, such as decreased blood flow to the brain, impaired peripheral vision or even losing consciousness.

Fighter pilots often experience g-forces in excess of five g's during high-speed turns in jet fighters. They wear a special g-suit that decreases some of the effects because it slows the blood flow by tightening down on the body extremities during the extreme loading. Or they have techniques such as bearing down to stave off the stress. But these corners normally last only a few seconds.

In 2001, the drivers in the CART race at Texas Motor Speedway were reaching as high as five g's and somewhat sustained through the banked corners. After drivers began complaining of dizziness after practice, the race was cancelled. It was determined there was a very high probability the continuous five-g corners at TMS would have created enough impairment to the drivers that crashing would occur.

LACTIC ACID ACCUMULATION

Lactic acid is, as the name suggests, an acid that builds up in the body during intense bouts of physical activity. One negative aspect of developing too much lactic acid is it causes fatigue. If the driver is involved in a race where the intensity causes lactic acid levels to rise, the fatigue could affect the driver's performance. We have measured lactic acid levels of drivers during testing in the race car, and also just as they stop the session and sit in the car. We have found lactic acid levels to rise significantly, thus demonstrating possible fatigue.

ELEVATED HEART RATE OXYGEN CONSUMPTION

When the human performs work, energy is needed to continue at the same levels. When you exercise, the heart rate rises to pump more oxygen-rich blood to the muscles and cardiovascular system. The race car driver experiences an increase in heart rate very similar to the levels of other sports.

While many feel the activity in the race car doesn't produce enough physical stress to compare to actual physical activity, research performed by Dr. Steve Olvey and Dr. Pat Jacobs with CART drivers showed the heart rate and oxygen consumption on a road course was similar to the amounts and levels of a long-distance swimmer, runner or professional cyclist.

PRESEASON FITNESS PREPARATION

Gaining an edge on the competition by improving fitness is an aspect every driver should take an interest in. Drivers from all levels of racing have discovered greater success in racing performance by following a structured fitness program. Before you get started, you need to understand the basic fitness components and why improving them will improve your driving skill.

ENDURANCE

At PitFit Training, we have measured heart rates as high as 196 beats per minute with a 29-year-old driver in a 125cc shifter kart. In similar research we have found an average of 170 beats per minute for a full 10-minute stint in the same type of kart. These were not overweight, out-of-shape drivers, but six healthy drivers in their 20s and 30s. These heart rates compare to those of competitive endurance athletes such as cyclists and runners. If you think racing karts does not heavily tax the cardiovascular system, think again. Then think of what it might be like if you progress to race big, heavy cars like Formula 1, stock cars or Indy Cars and have to keep up the pace for two hours or more.

STRENGTH

The idea of lifting weights to improve on-track performance may or may not surprise some drivers, especially Formula 1 and Indy Car drivers. Strength training, especially in the shoulder and torso region, will reduce the amount of fatigue felt as the race progresses, and allows the driver to maintain better control of the race car. It is apparent a driver lacks the strength to race at peak levels when they can't consistently stay in the proper groove in corners and begin missing apexes. These mistakes often cause a driver to lose positions in the closing laps.

REACTION TIMES

Many years ago, the U.S. military discovered that soldiers who played reaction-based video games performed better on combat drills requiring fast reflexes. Video games that require instant processing of thoughts train the brain in a similar fashion to what a driver experiences. Should you quit your job and saddle up next to the geek at the local game shop playing the latest edition of *Forza*? No, but playing games that stimulate the mind to process information and immediately react to this information might improve how well you react on the track.

FLEXIBILITY

One of the most controversial topics in modern sports conditioning is whether or not stretching positively affects athletic performance. Except in certain cases, we don't think it does. Research has shown an athlete should focus on warm-up motions similar to the sport in which they participate. Properly warming up a particular part of the body increases heat production, thus increasing the range of motion. One would be hard-pressed to find many sports asking the athlete to hold a position for 20–30 seconds followed by a rest period. Taking the body through a series of warm-up movements not only warms up the body, but also slowly raises the heart rate in a gradual manner. This gradual progression better prepares the athlete for the demands of competition. Without a warm-up, some blood that should be assisting with transporting much-needed oxygen to the lungs may instead be redirected to cold muscles. This occurs in an attempt to provide heat to cold connective tissue and muscles.

TESTING

What is testing? Testing is the repetitive analysis of performance in a controlled environment. In a race car, this data can then be used to determine progress and for making adjustments. If you would spend the money and time to go test your race car for a day, why would you not use the same scientific approach with your body?

Developing a simple fitness testing protocol will provide the driver a baseline of information on current fitness levels, as well as goals to work toward. Choose one or two basic tests from each category and retest yourself monthly to evaluate progress. It is important to follow the exact protocol precisely at each test.

KEY TRAINING AREAS

The driver should train the entire body during his program, with special emphasis on key areas.

• Neck: The stress from g-forces and bumpy tracks can cause a driver's neck muscles to fatigue significantly. When the neck becomes tired, a driver's vision can be negatively affected as his peripheral vision is relied upon more. Another reason to train the neck is injury prevention not only from driving, but from accidents that may occur. A strong neck has been shown to reduce the risk of concussion due to the decreased range of motion that occurs during impact. In the event there is a neck injury, maintaining strength in this area normally assists in the healing of muscles and connective tissue as well. However, it's important to understand that bulk does not necessarily mean race-fit strength. In Formula 1 in particular, the drivers have sufficient strength to withstand the rigors without having bulbous necks.

• Shoulders: The shoulders of a Formula 1 or Indy Car driver are instrumental in maintaining proper alignment of the steering position. When fatigued, the shoulders may not react as quickly to on-track situations, thus causing decreased performance. Because the position and driving demands of a driver emphasize muscles of the chest and front portion of the shoulders, focus on strengthening these areas is important. But the contrasting muscles in the upper back and rear shoulder area should also be trained to maintain balance and reduce injury risk.

• Core: Unlike most athletes who utilize core activity through multidirectional movement, the race car driver essentially has the stress of g-forces on the core. These are forces placed on him while immobilized in the cockpit with restraining harnesses. When the driver's core is strong, the muscles in the core region absorb these g-forces. This allows the muscles of the shoulders, arms and hands to efficiently perform the precise movement of steering with greater efficiency. However, when the core weakens, the g-forces begin to weaken the steering muscles much more, thus decreasing the ability to drive properly.

Another consideration is to train the core in a similar fashion to what the driver encounters while driving. A football or basketball player encounters a large amount of large-muscle movement during play, thus emphasis should be on performing dynamic core-strengthening exercises that simulate the sport. Training of the core for the race car driver should include a large amount or core stabilization training, where the core maintains a rigid structure while lifting a weight. The weight causes the core to tighten up, not necessarily have a lot of movement. This can be accomplished through balance-based exercises on some type of unstable surface, such as a foam pad or an Indo Board. Loading the muscles while on the unstable surface simulates the same situation as encountered in the race car.

• Arms/Forearms: Having a strong grip is a common trait of a race car driver. Without strength in the hands, forearms and arms, the driver has more difficulty steering with precision. The weaker these muscles are, the more likely a driver will grip the steering wheel too hard, which may lead to premature fatigue. Performing common exercises such as forearm curls, wrist rollers and squeezing a tennis ball will help provide strength in these areas. An activity we have found success with for strengthening these muscles is rock climbing. The constant clinging and climbing of tiny sections of rock forces one to maintain constant force on the gripping muscles, or risk falling! Indoor rock climbing gyms are found almost everywhere, and are a great way to train while having fun.

STAMINA TRAINING

To properly train your body to withstand the heart rate stress encountered when driving, you must try to simulate these same stresses in training. Performing reaction skills while the heart rate is elevated is also important, as this is precisely what occurs when making on-track decisions in a race.

There are numerous types of activities you can choose for cardiovascular training, but it's important you incorporate variety. While it's often comfortable to train in one activity, this increases the risk of overuse injuries. Try choosing one or two activities that stress opposing muscles of the lower body, such as biking and running, and one that focuses on the upper body, such as swimming or rowing.

In this phase of the training, I want you to focus on two specific training zones called Max Endurance and Short Interval.

• Max Endurance or ME: This is the foundation of your stamina training and consists of one to two hours of low-intensity training. The pace should be high enough to raise the heart rate to the 125–150 range, but not so high you can't finish the desired duration. It's best to do these with low-impact activities, such as cycling or an elliptical trainer in the gym. Perform ME workout two or three times per week.

• Short Interval or SI: This is a fairly short but intense series of bursts that raise the heart rate to the highest levels. Examples would be 100-meter sprints, 25 yards in the pool, etc. I only want you to do these one or two times weekly until more of a foundation of training is developed. Never do SI workouts on consecutive days.

REACTION TRAINING

Performing reaction-based drills is crucial to improving on-track performance. There are dozens of drills we do with our drivers, but the fundamental principle is they are performed while the driver is in a fatigued state. Rather than provide complicated exercises, focus on a simple activity you can combine with your ME workout. These might be juggling or card catch. It is advised you perform these drills at the end of your training session when fatigue is highest. This improves your ability to react in a fatigued state, similar to what is encountered in the car.

• Juggling: Start with one ball, and simply toss from one hand to the other. Repeat for one minute. Gradually work in a second ball, and, if you have the talent, a third. Doing this when you are fresh sounds easy. Try it after a hard workout when it's a struggle to hold your arms in front of you!

• Card Catch: Using a partner, have them drop playing cards from eye level. You must start with hands at your side, and alternate trying to catch the card before it gets to the ground.

I have known Jim Leo for many years and he has dedicated his life's work to making race cars drivers more fit. The areas above are some of the things that make training for race cars drivers a little different and a lot more specialized. When you get to a specialized level, you will need a specialized coach.

CHAPTER 7

DESIRE AND COMMITMENT

*A true champion needs the desire to chase
the dream through the most difficult times, the desire
to win at all costs and the desire to be the best
you can be at all times.*

I MENTIONED THE WORD "choice" earlier, as being one of the most powerful words in the English language. Let me reiterate, the greatest power we all possess is the power to choose: to choose whether we will make the big effort or not; to choose whether we want to emulate the work ethic of a Schumacher, Vettel, Alonso, Johnson, or some other driver who extracts the maximum from himself through dedication and application. You have probably heard this many times, but the simple fact is, with the window of opportunity being so small these days, if you don't at least emulate the efforts and drive of the known stars (or perhaps set new standards), you will not put yourself into as strong a position to be successful as you might. Plain and simply, this is where the rubber meets the road.

Imagine yourself sitting in front of Ferrari team manager Stefano Domenacalli, or McLaren principle Martin Whittmarsh, or NASCAR owner Rick Hendrick, or Roger Penske and telling him you just couldn't get something done. Feel the words leaving your lips, telling them the results were not there *because,* and that next year will be different. With the speed these teams move (especially in Formula 1) and the opportunity window closing more each weekend, your chances become more limiting with each excuse and each weak decision.

As we get to number six on the list of attributes needed for the Champion's Pyramid, we get to one of the final areas of separation between the champions and the pretenders.

We also get to the area that is essentially noncoachable. Everything discussed so far is teachable, learnable or coachable. The results of these activities are also visible in performance. When we moved from the quantifiable foundation of hard skill sets, to the soft skills, we move to an area unique to every driver. Desire is a measurement of a part of the driver's heart and soul. The heart is what produces the type of desire needed to chase a motorsports dream, or any dream for that matter. A true champion needs the desire to stick with it through the difficult times, the desire to want to win at all costs, the desire to want to be the best you can be at all times. The desire that no matter what happens or what anyone says, you will fight to the end to make it happen for you.

Although desire is not measurable with equipment, it is nevertheless measurable. Desire is not something you say, it's something you possess and therefore is seen in your behavior. Desire is a quality, and a behavior that is recognizable, and is a trait that is endearing. Drivers who show true desire tend to attract support from enthusiasts who like to be associated with them and want to support what they see as true desire. These are the type of relationships that can accelerate a career forward.

I once asked Mario Andretti what he believed was the most important thing a young driver needed when he set out to make it to the top. Was it talent, bravery, money, technical ability or none of the above? Mario looked me in the eye and uttered just one word: "Desire." Because motor-sports is such a hard business to succeed in, and there are so many hurdles to overcome, Mario believed the desire to be successful was the final attribute that separated the potential stars from the pretenders. He said hundreds of drivers would like to be successful, but only a small number had the desire to do whatever is necessary to chase the dream.

Strong desire to be successful often rubs people the wrong way. Strong desire needs to be surrounded by secure people, because they tend to understand the actions of people with strong desire. The so-called killer instinct present in most champions is very often what people call the actions of a person with a strong desire to win.

EUROPEAN MENTALITY

Having grown up with the European road-racing mentality and having lived through many struggles before finally making it to Formula 1, I believe I am in a position of authority to talk about desire. I have also experienced from both sides of the Atlantic Ocean how the American definition of desire differs from the European definition. Having spent the past 30 years racing and working in American motorsports, I have had reason to question the desire of some young American race car drivers. America as a country has always provided a surplus of activities for teen-agers, and in many cases this seems to have created a comfort zone that leads young hopefuls to question whether the effort and sacrifice is really worth it or not. Or, worse still, they don't actually know what true sacrifice really is.

Never forget, no one owes you anything. Life in general owes you nothing. You get what you deserve and you reach heights using steps on the ladder you yourself create. In racing terms, the comforts of home, and life in general, create a false floor suspended somewhere above reality and perception.

Consider this: Are you prepared to give up your comforts and social life to dedicate every waking hour to the betterment of your career? Are you prepared to work long hours with no thanks to help your career? Would you or your family be prepared to make alternate arrangements for your schooling if you had to spend extended time on the road? Would you or your family be prepared to forgo a college education to chase your dream of becoming a professional race car driver? These are all legitimate questions you need to be able to answer.

I had many weaknesses during my career, but desire and commitment was not one of them (remember I'm a Choleric). In 1974, I signed on as a laborer in an Iron Ore mine in Northwest Australia. It was the dirtiest, hardest, hottest and most enjoyable work I had ever experienced. Eight-hour shifts were the norm, but a 16-hour shift paid double-time for the second shift. A 24-hour shift added triple-time for the last eight hours. Everyone did his or her regular eight-hour shifts. A small group consistently volunteered for the double shifts, but a very small group of us volunteered for the 24-hour shift (there were no labor laws in the Australian outback in 1974). Every two weeks, while in the mess hall, we would have our private competitions with ourselves as we looked at our pay packets to see just how many hours we managed to book. The object of the exercise was to get as much money as possible in as short a period of time as possible. Six months later I had enough money to buy a Formula Ford and my career was underway.

In 1976 I lived in an old school bus and traveled from circuit to circuit in England while racing a Formula Ford. One day while driving along the main freeway, the M1, to a track in northern England, the diesel engine in the bus blew up. In one easy lesson, I learned all about grease, diesel and dirt as I rebuilt the engine, including having new valve seats fitted to the cylinder head and new crank-shaft bearings. This was all done in a rest area while the English weather soaked and chilled me to the bone.

Toward the end of the season in 1976, I had a throttle stick open, and the resulting high-speed crash destroyed my Formula Ford Hawke DL15. I was so frightened by the impact that I collapsed when I was lifted from the car. My left leg was heavily bruised, I had suffered permanent muscle damage and I had to have it in a cast-like dressing for three weeks. Two days after the crash, and despite the considerable pain, I was in the factory cutting and welding my chassis, because that was the only way I could get back on the track. I lived outside the factory in the car park by myself. The days were long and sometimes lonely, but giving up would have been the easy option.

At the race tracks each week, I would swap similar stories with other drivers from Brazil or France or wherever, drivers who were trying to achieve the same goals I was striving for. Despite our friendships, we would tear each other apart on the race track, because winning was everything to a small, dedicated group from across the globe.

British Journalist Mark Hughes wrote the following about the great British former world champion Nigel Mansell. He was prompted to write this after again experiencing Mansell's desire and commitment to the Grand Prix Masters championship, when Nigel was the other side of the 50-year mark:

"A top F1 driver is a mass of competitive drives. Talent, while the number-one prerequisite, is nowhere near enough on its own.

"To that basic baseline he needs to add supreme fitness and raw primeval desire or hunger. He has to want very badly to do it; the need to compete has to be hard-wired into him. The fitness levels won't normally interest him on an abstract level, but are a means to an end, and, as such, he's driven to achieve them. Not only will it help him physically in the car, but the spare mental capacity the fitness buys him will enable him to compete far more effectively.

"The desire factor is a fascinating one. The intensity of it is all that marks out a great driver from a good one. When Nigel Mansell was in a race car he wrung the neck of his own abilities every time he sat in the car, driven to a degree that sometimes bordered on insanity. With a rival in his sights, you knew something was going to happen, either he'd pull off the big move, or there would be an incident. It sent a shiver down the spine. Who knows what drove him to such a place."

Mark remains convinced a very big part of what made Mansell the driver he was, was showing the racing world just how wrong it had got him—proving the bastards wrong while at the same time lapping up the adulation of Mansellmania, taking great satisfaction from how people with no knowledge of the sport had seen what the racing world still struggled to see—that he was a very great driver indeed.

That drive and desire was still evident as the Grand Prix Masters championship unfolded in 2005. Mark also reasoned it was difficult to see anyone else on the entry list of Grand Prix Masters that would be able to match Mansell's exceptional drive and desire. Has anyone ever said that about you, or will someone ever make that comment about you in the future?

I often wonder if the same desire is alive and well today. Has today's society changed the way we think about what type of effort should be expected to achieve anything significant?

AMERICAN MENTALITY

In 1984, Rick Mears and I were in Methodist Hospital in Indianapolis. Unfortunately, we were both recovering from devastating injuries from two Indy Car crashes two weeks apart. We both had smashed feet and ankles and significant other orthopedic injuries that required multiple surgeries with bone and skin grafting. I had some 14 different surgeries and Rick had even more. The therapy alone just to walk again was a minimum of two years.

After a two-month stay in the hospital, I was discharged to a rehabilitation center. Before I left I wheeled my wheelchair into Rick's room and asked him if he thought he would ever race again. He paused, looked me in the eye and told me he would, because the same desire to race he had prior to the devastating injuries was still burning within him. I told him I still remembered the day I told my dad, when I was 12, that I wanted to be a race car driver, and that the accident was not the legacy I wanted to leave in the sport. We both went back to the sport that almost killed us and both won the biggest races of our careers after the accidents.

Today's model is a little different, but still very similar at the same time. In 2011, Mark Hughes wrote the following about Sebastian Vettel: "The outside world only rarely gets to see the intense greed for success that fuels Vettel's performances. But the crew certainly get to see it when something goes wrong. He's got an almost animalistic fury, particularly when he feels he has allowed something achievable out of his grasp. It's a trait of most of the top sporting athletes throughout history. It's a stark contrast to his normally sunny demeanor, but there's no conflict in that fact; it's merely a betrayal of the force that drives him forward. It's used and directed by that keen intellect, and together with his physical skills it makes him a totally formidable competitor. This is desire to be the best in its raw form."

Think about what might happen if you add a strong work ethic to strong desire. Five-time NASCAR championship-winning crew chief Chad Knaus offered that Jimmie is charting new territory in NASCAR, and that's due to a combination of natural talent and unsurpassed work ethic.

Nico Hulkenberg stated, "If you want to beat them, you have to learn quicker and work harder. I think we were pretty good with that." Would anyone disagree that both Johnson and Hulkenberg show clear signs of having strong desire and have a red-lined work ethic to go along with it? What a toolbox!

GOLDEN OPPORTUNITY SQUANDERED

During the Team Green Academy Driver Development program in 1996–1997 we had several examples of what I call "pure desire to succeed," and then an unfortunate example of what I termed as "dud desire."

One of the drivers to come through our program was Paul Edwards. Paul was very quick, very determined, but most of all he had a great heart and passion for what he was doing and a great desire to succeed.

Paul left his home comforts, left his enviable California lifestyle and lived like a gypsy in England, knocking on all doors that might help him in his quest to become a professional race car driver. How many drivers do you know who would give up all the knowns about their lifestyle and plunge into the uncertainty of the unknowns in a country half a world away?

After years in Formula Fords, Paul eventually made it to the British Formula 3 championship. The British Formula 3 championship has a habit of developing Formula 1 drivers, but, alas, Paul's efforts collapsed halfway through the season because of lack of adequate funding. At all times, though, Paul showed the type of desire that Mario Andretti talked about, and it eventually paid off for Paul, perhaps because he became a paid professional in the sedan and sports car ranks.

By contrast, Team Green Academy winner Jeff Shafer was the epitome of a young driver who had everything he needed to be a champion, except a strong enough desire to overcome the distractions of his circumstances. I still believe today Jeff was on his way to being a very successful professional race car driver with the world at his feet. It was not to be, however, because of that missing magic ingredient that Mario Andretti fully understands, desire. It still pains me to say it, but I believe it was the epitome of a golden opportunity squandered.

At the end of 1997, Brown & Williamson pulled the plug of the driver development program and I decided to manage Jeff's career. The first thing was to get him some stability, and I managed to negotiate a five-year contract with Forsythe Racing. Because he had not done many races the year before, it was decided to send him to Europe for the Palmer Audi series for several reasons. He would get to race 19 times, he would have to adapt to a new culture, learn all-new tracks and race against the European road-racing mentality.

To help keep his profile high in the United States while he raced in Europe, we arranged for Jeff to have his own driver's column in *On Track* magazine (America's motorsports magazine at the time). I then started discussions with Speedvision about televising the Palmer Audi series in the states with a special American focus featuring Jeff at every race. To keep him happy while he played on the water while home in Las Vegas, Jeff also had a contract with Bombardier Sea Doo that supplied him his water toys. Jeff was also paid a significant salary that year, which I believe made him the highest paid fringe professional in England that year.

After Jeff's first test sessions at Snetterton in England, he was within 0.1 second of the fastest driver. Series owner Jonathan Palmer called me himself to state how impressive he thought Jeff was. He was saying how good it might be for his series to have an American possibly win it.

While I was setting all of this up, I called two friends of mine who were managing drivers. One was my former teammate at Williams in 1982, Keke Rosberg, who was managing Mika Hakkinen. The other was David Sears, who ran the most successful Formula 3000 race team in Europe, who managed drivers such as Juan Montoya, Bruno Junqueira and Sebastien Bourdais. They helped me structure a fair contract that called for no payment from Jeff until he started earning enough to pay a management fee. The last thing I did was set-up a company for him and secured a trusted money manager.

About three races into the season I began to get alarmed by some of Jeff's actions, or should I say his lack of actions. I had arranged for him to drive the factory BMW M3 in the American Le Mans event at the Las Vegas Motor Speedway on one of his off weekends from England. I assumed he would grab the opportunity with both hands, be present at all times, make himself useful whenever possible and generally begin to show his desire. Instead of being in the pit lane during practice sessions, Jeff was on nearby Lake Meade fixing some boat engine. Now Jeff was a very laid-back California boy (Phlegmatic) who always walked to the beat of his own drum, and this was one of his endearing qualities, but a total disregard for getting to know the cars and people when they were under his nose alarmed me.

More alarm bells went off almost immediately. The living accommodations in England were not good enough for him and his new wife. Living in England seemed to be hard for them. Instead of it being a great adventure that would create the foundation where his career would stand, it became a burden.

Jeff got married, started a family and dedicated his life to something other than being a race car driver. I canceled my management agreement with him. Forsythe Racing fulfilled their obligation until the end of the year and then terminated his contract.

I was personally bewildered by his actions, and I then asked myself the hard question: Do American drivers really have the desire it takes to become successful as a race car driver? Jeff Shafer had desire, but it was not directed at becoming a professional race car driver.

How many teen-agers do you currently know who drive all over this country to race? Long days and nights of inconvenience on the road, sleeping in cars or trucks on nonstop trips and viewing the sunrise from their vehicle more than once on the same trip. How long will it last for some of them? When will some of them just tire of the grind? How many of these teen-agers can separate the want to race as opposed to the need to race? Want and need are what separate the true desire from the pretender. Make no mistake about it, a career in motorsports will be tough, demanding and more than most people can cope with. You will be beaten down, told no, rejected and just plain abused by your competitors, and sometimes by your family. You will have bad days and then even worse days. You will ask yourself if it is all worth it. Your maturity level will be tested and you will be forced to grow up rapidly.

Do you want to race for yourself or for someone else? Are you doing this for yourself or for your family? If it all stopped in the morning, would you miss it? Hidden behind all these questions is the answer to whether you have the desire or not to pursue the big time.

In 1990 I won the prestigious Sebring 12-Hour race driving the dominant car of the time, the Nissan GTP ZX Turbo. It was a very satisfying win, because I ended up driving almost eight hours of the race. It had been close to 11 years since my last international win of significance. During those 11 years, I had pushed as hard as ever to get to the top of the rostrum. However, having reached the top, the feeling when I got there was just not what I had expected. The sense of satisfaction just did not seem to give me the buzz I was expecting. I very quickly realized that for me, at that time of my life and career, the search for success behind the wheel of a race car no longer held the same significance.

That was the day I knew my desire to continue to dedicate my life to driving racing cars was beginning to change. The will to push myself both physically and mentally every day was no longer as strong as when I drove Formula 1 or Indy Cars. I knew the Sebring win was the beginning of the end of my driving career. Just over two years later I walked away from the only life I had ever known.

If you are presented with opportunities, will you be prepared to make the sacrifices? Are your comforts too comfortable? Can you get comfortable being uncomfortable?

Would you leave your comforts of home and move to Japan like former Ferrari driver Eddie Irvine did to continue growing your career? Do you know what the difference is between making an emotional decision versus a heart-driven decision? The heart-driven decisions are the measure of a driver's desire. When desire is abundant, it's amazing the amount of people who appear and want to help with the cause. Are you in a position to put yourself in that position?

COMMITMENT

Hand in hand with desire is commitment, which is also a noncoachable character trait. You can't make someone commit. You can tell them what might happen if they did certain things, but you can't make people do things they decide they don't want to do themselves. More often than not the complete champions commit and focus to the exclusion of outside distractions to the point where they can become curt, abrupt or sometimes rude. Those committed to success sometimes react badly to outside distractions invading their controlled space.

Just like desire, commitment is quantifiable, but not through analogue or digital measurement. Without true commitment, it is doubtful many successful drivers would have made it to the top. Commitment is doing whatever it takes and having that can-do attitude. It could also be described as work ethic. Different work ethics among different drivers is easy to recognize.

Every help-wanted ad in specialty motorsports magazines seeking employees for top-flight teams has an automatic filter for respondents. In their ads they specifically ask if you are highly capable, innovative, self-motivated, result-orientated, stress tolerant and dedicated. Those are all words that weed out those who would not fit a winning team culture. If these are the desired employees, do you think similar traits are also desired from drivers? There are exceptions to every rule, such as the low-wattage Kimi Raikkonen, but he would not be considered as a model for most teams I know.

True commitment is like a vow, and that vow will be seriously challenged many times along the journey. What separates those who stay true to their personal commitment is also what separates the ones who can persevere through the pain and frustrations of motor racing's very challenging obstacle course.

There can be different levels of commitment. What one considers as a great deal of commitment another might consider being just average.

Nico Rosberg and Lewis Hamilton were teammates in the European Formula A karting championship in 2000 in a Mercedes-backed team operated by Dino Chiesa. They finished first and second in that championship with Lewis just edging out Rosberg. Chiesa said it wasn't talent that separated them as they were evenly matched. "They were both very fast and could make good decisions," he said.

But, he added, "if there was one thing separating them it was Lewis' fighting attitude. He would take risks to win whereas Nico always had an eye on finishing. Lewis usually wins his fights and it's something you are born with. You cannot tell a driver to be more aggressive." Interesting words from a master of karting who has handled some of the world's best drivers.

It was also written that when Rosberg was at Williams, the team slowly fell out of love with him. The team rated his talent highly, but not his application, or commitment. There was a feeling he was too easy on himself, didn't push himself hard enough to be better. He would dismiss his trainer's requests to work harder at the gym. For example, he had a habit of setting the running machine on a low number and reading while running.

So this is part of what the world's media are saying for everyone to see, hear and absorb. This opinion may or may not be accurate. It will be interesting to see this play out during Rosberg's Formula 1 career, or perhaps it already has.

Consider what Michael Schumacher said after he retired from competition for the first time in response to criticism of his often controversial driving style. In England's *Autosport* magazine the following report appeared. Michael said he could not argue with observers and fellow drivers who labeled him "selfish" over 15 years in Formula 1. "I agree with that," he said. "Why should I gift anything to anyone when we're on the track?"

Schumacher's career was punctuated by moments of controversial driving, including the clash with Damon Hill at the 1994 Australian Grand Prix that decided the world championship in his favor. He also hit Jacques Villeneuve at the 1997 European Grand Prix that resulted in Schumacher's retirement and Villeneuve becoming world champion. Perhaps one of his most controversial moments might have been his bungled attempt to disrupt the last moments of qualifying in Monaco in 2006 when Alonso was slowed while attempting to take the all-important pole position.

To these accusations, Michael simply suggested his detractors were just misguided: "To be honest, if the other drivers criticize me, then it means I've done things the right way." Bold, defiant and unflinching. This is real glimpse into the mind of a committed champion.

After Massa's accident in Hungary, when an errant spring from Barrichello's car struck his helmet just above the visor resulting in serious head injuries, a new nylon visor strip that added an additional layer of protection was introduced. Although not made mandatory, the FIA made it clear it would like all drivers to consider wearing it. I was the driver steward at Monza that day in 2011 and during the driver's meeting a defiant Michael Schumacher made it clear to the FIA chief steward Charlie Whiting that he and he alone would make the decision on what safety devices he would use if they were not mandatory. Even though his skills may have been somewhat blunted because of the passing years and his three-year break, it was interesting to see that his cold, hard, defiant, purposeful and focused self was still intact.

Another view comes from Jenson Button after he joined BAR Honda in 2003: "I soon realized that I needed to devote every single second of my time to the team, and to learn. You're never the complete driver; even now, I'm always learning. I don't beat myself up riding up mountains for nothing; the end goal is to be the fittest driver in F1, because it gives me a little edge. Maybe it doesn't make a physical difference, but mentally it does. Maybe that's not true for other drivers, but it is for me, and that's what matters. I'm giving everything I've got, and I don't think there's any area I'm lacking in at the moment." This is the type of work ethic and commitment that allowed him to become world champion in 2009, and establish himself as a complete driver at McLaren, even with Lewis Hamilton as his teammate.

Few would argue three-time world champion Sebastian Vettel isn't committed to perfection. Red Bull's driver program director Dr. Helmut Marko has described Vettel as a pain in the ass.

"He's not easy to work with because he is so demanding," Dr. Marko says. "He knows how he wants things and he makes sure he gets them how he wants. Because as far as he is concerned, these are all steps toward his goal of winning the world championship. He's not interested in making friends; he's interested in progressing toward this goal. And he's become even more demanding as he has tasted success."

It's a known fact that if Vettel has a weakness, he is committed to quickly understanding it and then he goes and fixes it. He is always demanding because of his burning desire and commitment.

What about the cultural backgrounds of drivers? Could a cultural background somehow breed the desire to succeed in one nation more so than in another? Your desire to do something is then complimented by your commitment to get it done. You might want to be a champion and might visualize yourself celebrating on the rostrum, but no matter what your desire is, it will go nowhere unless you have the commitment to do whatever it takes to make it happen. You have heard that when the going gets tough the tough get going. It has never been so true for race car drivers. Motor racing will test your resolve unlike any other sport. Your success is not usually determined by your level of talent. There are many variables that depend on the strengths of many others that you must depend on before you can display your talents. Seldom do all these forces work in harmony or consistently when a driver is in his formative years. Frustration can be considered to be a filter that separates whole-hearted versus half-hearted commitment. Always remember that the only place where *success* comes before *work* is in the dictionary.

Indy Car's Will Power is an interesting driver if only because of what he has not won (as of 2012). As a member of the powerful Team Penske Indy Car team, he has had access to what is arguably the best equipment and support a driver could have, yet he has failed to win the championship (as of this writing). Part of what distinguishes him is his uncanny ability to go fast and save fuel at the same time. He is a great listener and is forever looking at what others are doing to see what he can learn from them. Penske Team Manager Tim Cindric, however, provides an interesting perspective on Power and how he goes about his racing.

Cindric says, "Will is one of the most complete drivers I have ever worked with. His general preparation is probably the best I have ever seen and he is open to learning at a level higher than most. He is forever asking questions and seeking advice, usually starting the week before a race. Usually drivers at his level are a little closed-minded to their weaknesses, but not Will. He is very open about any weakness and immediately looks to gather information to help him in whatever way possible. He will often send people to observe at particular corners if he needs additional information to get faster." This sounds to me like a driver pretty driven and committed to being the very best he can be.

A great example of what was deemed by the European media to be a weak commitment was Michael Andretti's attempt to become established in Formula 1 with McLaren in 1993. Michael had proven to the world he was very gifted and had risen to the top of Indy Car racing in America. He had signed with McLaren as teammate to the great Ayrton Senna. I traveled the world that year covering Michael's every move for ESPN television. One of the reasons I became intrigued by his failure was that I believed, and still do, he was one of the most talented drivers in the world, yet it appeared that he had one missing ingredient from the Champion's Pyramid that year: commitment.

As I watched Michael during practice and qualifying sessions, I saw a driver who did not drive with the flamboyant, loose style I knew he possessed. He looked awkward and did not seem to fit the car or team. His timing was off and the fluid, confident style he had developed was somehow suppressed.

Because Formula 1 was a lifestyle as opposed to a sport, a doubting eye was cast Michaels' way when he decided not to move to Europe, but instead continue to live in Nazareth, PA. He would then use the family plane to get him to New York airport, where he would board Concord for the trans-Atlantic flight. The comforts of home it would appear were more important to him than being closer to the team in England.

This was a challenging time for McLaren, as it had lost its factory engine deal and had replaced it with a customer Ford Cosworth engine. It was also a time when the rules of Formula 1 changed, allowing only 12 laps of practice per session. These two moves stacked the odds against Michael immediately and made his transition even more difficult. His teammate proved, however, the engine situation did not create insurmountable odds. At least Senna seemed to recognize Michael's talent and was a consistent supporter of his within the team.

The season did not start off well, with an engine stall on the grid in South Africa. It went from bad to worse with many first-lap crashes. At a time when the team was frustrated with Michael's performance, there was a feeling within the team that instead of working through the issues with the team, Michael retreated to the comforts of home. The team viewed this as a lack of commitment.

The commitment you make to a team will probably determine the commitment they make to you. It is my belief that by Michael not making the lifestyle commitment to live in Europe sent a message to the team he was not prepared to make the necessary sacrifice. I believe his lack of a total commitment, whether it was perceived or not, was felt by McLaren, and I believe their commitment to him was in turn weak, and the spiral started to go downhill from there.

Many years later, American journalist Matt Davis wrote an interesting story which highlighted Michael's plight, and then posed some questions that highlighted the cultural backgrounds:

"The last American F1 driver was Michael Andretti in 1993—a terrible season with McLaren-Ford in which Andretti showed absolutely no sign of wanting to commit to the rarefied atmosphere of international Formula car racing. He'd fly in for each race and fly back to Pennsylvania immediately afterward, making almost no effort to ingratiate himself with his fellow crew members. Which was fine by one Mika Hakkinen, who jumped into Andretti's seat before it even had a chance to cool, going on to do pretty well, I'd say. [Mika Hakkinen went on to become a two-time world champion.]

"So what's preventing America and American drivers from getting into the Formula 1 scene?"

Talking with broadcast legend Chris Economaki and some European journalists, here's some of what came up in Davis' conversations:

"American drivers aren't hungry enough. In fact, they're lazy by European standards."

"American drivers expect to make money almost immediately, whereas drivers on the international circuit invest for years out of love for the sport and feel blessed if they break even."

"American drivers do not live and work outside of America easily, struggling to accept the cultural and attitudinal differences that are the reality of being away from home."

"American drivers are great once the tires are hot and grippy, but are terrible during qualifying runs on fresh slicks."

"American drivers in series outside the United States almost always blame the equipment, crew and/or other drivers for everything that goes wrong instead of diving in, pinpointing the real source of the problem and addressing it."

"Not all of these are unique to us, certainly, but where does this leave us? Not an easy one to answer. Are we incurable homebodies incapable of leaving the nest and taking on multiple struggles behind the wheel in foreign lands? Ugly Americans? Some would say yes."

I believe this type of story, although relevant in some areas, misses the point. The reason Michael failed is because it appears his commitment level did not nearly match his talent level.

For whatever reason, the above included, Michael's quest failed. Even though it might have been difficult, the cold, hard fact is it was generally perceived he didn't do whatever it took. This was an example of one of the world's most talented drivers not quite having all the pieces of the Champion's Pyramid needed to succeed in the environment he was in. In McLaren's eyes, they just said he wasn't good enough, which to this day I believe was wrong.

The other Michael—Schumacher—was the complete opposite. He oozed commitment. Commitment was a way of life for Schumacher. Commitment was a habit for him. *Autosport*'s Nigel Roebuck once wrote, "Michael earns the respect of all the people around him: people know he's committed, and doing the best job he can, so naturally everyone around him does the same—you don't have to motivate people very much when Michael's around."

If Formula 1 is to be regarded as the pinnacle of motor-sports in the world, perhaps references to some of its stars would also be relevant. Who are and were the dedicated hard workers in Formula 1? Alain Prost worked hard at his craft. Ayrton Senna poured over data for hours on race weekends, and of course more recently Michael Schumacher was regarded as the hardest worker of them all.

When Schumacher retired from Ferrari, everybody considered Kimi Raikkonen to be arguably the fastest man in Formula 1 and therefore a worthy replacement. It was interesting to read the comments about Kimi from the professionals who either worked with or alongside Michael.

Former Jordan designer Gary Anderson was even concerned about the knock-on effect to a teammate when a driver with such high work ethics departs. He said, "Kimi has a different work ethic from Michael and it will be interesting to see how Felipe Massa responds to that. With Michael there, you had the impression that he worked hard because Michael was the benchmark. Without Michael, that will change."

Again after Michael retired, a journalist I respect greatly, Jonathan Noble, wrote a very interesting story in *Racer* magazine. He cited a Formula 1 team manager who did not want to be named as saying, "Kimi is absolutely magical. He is the kind of talent that you see only once in 10 or 15 years." He then wondered how he had missed him as he rose through the lower formulae. He said, "Kimi had amazing speed, that he lived to drive Formula 1 cars on the absolute limit." What he then said was what caught my attention: "Kimi would never become a champion at Ferrari unless he changed the brain in his head. He was nowhere near Michael when it comes to commitment application to the job and just working hard. It's sad, but it's true."

This statement ended up being correct. Ferrari fired him because he became measured by what they determined to be his commitment or lack thereof, and Ferrari was not prepared to structure the team environment around Kimi's needs like Lotus did upon his comeback to Formula 1 in 2012.

Commitment can be a huge assist to a drivers' development, but let's remember that right in the front of this book we determined every driver is unique in how he operates. Let me give you an example of going against the grain and it working successfully. Raikkonen was fired by Ferrari for what they determined to be subpar commitment. Kimi, however, determined his commitment was good enough and all he needed was a team who understood him and would provide him with the right environment, an environment that would effectively fill the perceived lack of commitment void. That environment was not Ferrari.

In 2007, Mark Hughes followed Kimi at Ferrari pretty closely, saying, "With Kimi, everything is in the doing, not the saying. He's undemanding, very relaxed—and so the initiative has to come from the team. But when they do that, he responds. But with Kimi they realize they need to pull the process along, whereas with Michael Schumacher it was almost impossible to feel the distinction between him pushing them and they pulling him."

Raikkonen proved his point when he returned to Formula 1 with Lotus in 2012. He didn't want to lead the team and his commitment was good enough in his mind to win. Lotus embraced his slow-burn, low-watt quirks along with his lack of interest in public relations, long meetings, bureaucracy or politics. He wanted a simple lifestyle that allowed him to just drive the car as fast as he could.

Eric Boullier, team manager of Team Lotus, must have taken note of the Ferrari issues, because the environment Lotus created around Kimi upon his return was one he flourished in. I'm not sure I've seen another Formula 1 team that understands what environment management means, especially when it pertains to a driver's quirky requirements.

How many drivers do you know with the same type of commitment as a Michael Schumacher, or an Alonso, or Vettel? Do you personally have the type of commitment needed to make it to the very top? Will your personal commitment help or hinder your career? Is there any truth in the above story? Does a cultural background make any difference?

DRIVERS WITH THE CHAMPION'S PYRAMID

The Champion's Pyramid is a bit like a house. It might look similar to the one beside it, but everything is, in fact, just a little different. Every champion has a different version of the Champion's Pyramid. In years past a Champion's Pyramid looked different because, for one, the physical preparedness was nowhere near the level it has become in this day and age. Just like all other sports played out on a world stage, every year that passes makes each sport more and more specialized. In years to come we will probably marvel at the lengths champions go to be the best they can be. Michael Schumacher's blood tests during test sessions to accurately evaluate his fitness levels, although leading edge at the time, might seem archaic in the years to come.

If you think from reading this book I am a big fan of Senna and Schumacher, you would be correct. You can see how easy it is to add Vettel and Alonso to the favorites list. I do still think, however, Schumacher is the most complete race car driver ever. Among others who have built or are building a Champion's Pyramid would be Jackie Stewart, Lewis Hamilton, Jeff Gordon, Alain Prost, Scott Dixon, Michael Andretti, Mario Andretti, Gil de Ferran, Sebastien Bourdais, Dale Earnhardt, Will Power and Dario Franchitti.

Fernando Alonso is an interesting study, as he appeared to get even better when he joined Ferrari. He was already a two-time world champion, but the emotional injection of driving for the great Italian scuderia has pushed him to even newer heights. Here are some comments made by the men closest to him on the championship-winning Renault team. Consider that these comments were made after he won the first of his world championships.

Executive Director of Engineering Pat Symonds said, "I think the main thing Fernando has, and which every champion needs, is intelligence. I won't say he won his championship by driving tactically, but he assured himself of the championship by driving tactically. What he did was very carefully control himself, and do what he needed to do to get the championship. And that shows a lot of maturity and restraint.

"There were times when I'd argue that his restraint was almost a little too much, and I felt that we could race a little bit harder. But, he does have this very deep understanding of how to go racing. He is remarkably good at understanding what's going on in the race, what needs to be done, reading the race, and exploiting it well. It really is one of his strengths, and it's a strength he shares with the other two champions I've worked with, Ayrton Senna and Michael Schumacher. If a guy drives a car and comes into the pits and doesn't know why he's gone quick or what the hell's going on, he's really at a disadvantage. There are some like that, but Fernando is not like that at all.

"A trait of great drivers is to adapt. A driver needs to work hard on the setups of his car for as long as he can, but there comes a time on Sunday when that's it, that's what you've got ... and that might even change if it rains.

"His technical understanding is good enough. I don't want engineers driving the car. I want people who can report honestly and accurately what's going on, and if they can't say, they can't. One of the things I like about Fernando is that if you make a change on the car and he can't feel it, he says it feels the same. He doesn't give you a long spiel.

"His race craft improves all the time, his maturity comes on. I don't think he can drive any faster now than when he started, I think that is sort of fixed. I think it's the understanding that improves. And he does work very hard at it now.

"If you ask where can he improve, I couldn't tell you. What I suspect is that he is 95, 97 or 99 percent. He certainly doesn't have any weaknesses that he needs to address."

The above statements by the men closest to him (at the time of his first world championship win) show Alonso has a mix of feel *sensitive-talent* (can engineer the car) and *instinct-reflex* talent (can drive it really fast). He can also communicate well and has great mental skills. He is obviously fit enough to drive Formula 1 cars for the course of a race distance, and most of all he displays the desire and commitment to chase his dream and be the very best he can be. The above statements by the people closest to his working environment show he probably has his personal Champion's Pyramid very well developed—not fully because we never stop learning. The above was written about Alonso in 2005. Back then he exhibited the traits and skills of a champion. Since then he has added more knowledge and experience and is even more complete.

More than anything else I want you to understand Alonso's habits and actions kept positioning him to be more successful than his competition.

THE VERY BEST

Although there are many great examples of drivers who have well-developed and mature Champion's Pyramids, few would disagree that if you were to model yourself and understand what it really takes to become truly successful in the sophisticated era we are now in, you should look hard at the career of Michael Schumacher. Alonso, Vettel, Hamilton, Button and Will Power are all elite athletes, but it is a fair argument Michael Schumacher had just that little bit more during his great years of success. He operated at a higher level because he worked harder, smarter and deeper than everyone else. The technical directors of his two championship-winning teams, Ross Brawn from Ferrari and Pat Symonds from Renault, were united in their assess-ment of Michael, saying he motivates and inspires people within the teams. He brings everybody together unlike anybody in the sport before him. He became the beacon by example, and everyone became willing followers because of his actions.

His on-track performance was what inspired his teams more than anything else, but it was his off-track habits that brought him the trophies and accolades. In motorsports, team members will work day and night for a driver who gives every ounce in and out of the race car. From Day One in a Formula 1 car, to the last day of his first career stint, he drove every lap and every corner like a qualifying lap, and 16 years after he first entered Formula 1 he was still driving every lap the same way, setting fastest race lap in his last race of career number-one at the Brazilian Grand Prix. After a three-year layoff and 20 years in the sport, and although his return to the cockpit was not as successful as he had hoped, he was still able to set a time fast enough for the pole in Monaco in his final season. That commitment to bring your A game every day is part of what inspires teams to be the very best they can be.

Speed TV's Formula 1 announcer Bob Varsha probably put it best when he said, "Michael was a selfish opportunist who never criticized his team, and a driver who reset the standards by which those who will follow will be judged. That ruthless driver obliterated every race record of note with 68 poles and 91 victories in 16 glorious seasons." There is no doubt that Michael Schumacher had the most fully developed Champion's Pyramid ever.

How many drivers in the past have ever separated themselves from the rest with this type of quality commitment? How many drivers in the future will do so? Are you a driver with these qualities? Would you like to have these qualities? Are you a driver prepared to make the needed commitment? If your parents or a sponsor are prepared to finance your opportunity, what type of path would you take toward developing into a champion? What sort of team of people would you gather around you to help you develop the needed skills? What would you personally do to develop all of the qualities of the Champion's Pyramid? Who would assemble your personal team of coaches that would help position you for success? Only you can answer those questions, and your answers will determine how high you fly.

EPILOGUE

IT IS A WELL-KNOWN FACT you are more than halfway to solving a problem when you identify it. Becoming a motorsports champion highlights many problems, and I hope I have given you some of the answers to the issues that face most drivers. Large team budgets are sometimes wasted because the foundation is not solid and the execution of the job at hand is not carried out efficiently or effectively. Ex-karter Michael Schumacher has proven the most successful teams are led by the driver.

Within the pages of this book, I have given you a key to a big door. The next step is for you to walk through the door yourself. However, to get through the door, you have to cross a threshold of terrain that requires specific skills and dedication. If you were not naturally blessed with all the skills required for a champion, it is my belief you can acquire them. I believe world champions Nigel Mansell, Damon Hill and Graham Hill would agree. So also would

Indy 500 champion Eddie Cheever. These are all drivers who worked at developing the skills necessary to be successful.

What you learn on the race track can be termed as the tangible part. What you learn away from the track can be the intangible. I promise you the intangible will be the difference between the amount of hardware you will actually have in your trophy cabinet and the amount you might have had.

The autobiographies of great champions are littered with stories of struggle, pain and sometimes despair. In an era where motorsports has become so specialized, becoming a professional race car driver while attending high school or college might be almost impossible. Successful motorsports is not just a passion, it's a lifestyle. It is a dedication of one's life to the requirements of the career. It is a selfish pursuit where relationships sometimes suffer and understanding partners are almost impossible to find. It is a colorful, glamorous, savage sport of gladiators who sometimes pay the ultimate price with their lives.

It is an emotionally charged atmosphere where the chase has sometimes left the pursuers both emotionally and financially bankrupt.

It is also one of the world's most satisfying endeavors. The physical difficulties and sacrifices are dwarfed by the golden satisfaction of competition and success. When a driver's talent is exposed and the decision making is tested to the fullest, and the adrenalin fills the veins through a pounding heart, being first to the finish is everything.

The road has now been laid out for you. Now it's up to you to start making your way forward. Are you ready to make that choice? If you say, "Yes," your life will change. How you live your life will change. How you view yourself and how others view you will change. You will think and act differently. My challenge to you is this: In your own very personal, private, quiet time, ask yourself if are you ready to make the choices that can build your own Champion's Pyramid. If the answer is, "Yes," then follow the guidelines.

Focus on the process, not the prize. Focus on being a champion rather than on becoming one. Fill your mind with good, wholesome thoughts. You have 100 percent control over what you think and the things you choose to do. Remember that powerful word "choice." The greatest power we all possess is the *power* to choose. Choose how we want to live, choose how much effort to put in. Choose what to do, say, see and learn.

One of my favorite sayings is something I heard many years ago in Las Vegas, that there is a book on just about everything. If you bet on a horse, there will be a book of information on every detail of the horse. There is a book about every race driver also. Mark Hughes contrasted the book of the top Formula 1 drivers at the end of 2010. Lewis Hamilton was the brilliant but mercurial guy sometimes blinded by red mist. Sebastian Vettel was always on the edge from the moment he braked for a corner, but with an occasional short circuit of petulance. His teammate Mark Webber was a hugely formidable competitor who sometimes wanted it just too much. Jenson Button had the purest driving style of all, but sometimes found it difficult to improvise around a car problem. Fernando Alonso possesses relentless brilliance, but with a psychological flaw that can be found if put under enough pressure.

Who is the fastest? Hamilton (but not technically strong). The smartest? Button (but not prepared to drive an unstable car). The most cunning? Alonso (but became emotionally unglued when paired with Hamilton). The toughest in battle? Webber (but unable to adapt to the Red Bull). The most adaptable? Vettel (but makes too many mistakes). Amazingly, every driver is ultimately categorized. They all have strengths and weaknesses. But who will get more of the success qualities aligned on any given day than his competition?

If someone wrote a book about you, what would that book say? After you spend several years in race paddocks, everyone in that paddock will know everything about you. They will know all of your strengths and weaknesses. Will they say you tried hard or that you were driven to be successful? Will they glow when describing your desire to be a champion? Will they say you worked hard at learning all of the skills needed to become a complete champion? You and you alone will sow the seeds of your future. You and you alone will have control of what they will say. What would you like them to say? Remember, we do not attract what we want, we attract what we are.

Strive to be a champion in the way you lead your life, not just in how you approach your racing. This will ultimately demand a mature, solid and confident mindset that keeps things in perspective. Remember what confidence is about, because it shouldn't be about an outcome. Rather, it should be about a strong inner belief, an unshakable knowledge— that no matter how big the challenge, no matter how tough the going gets, that you can count on yourself to bring the best you've got to every performance. To consistently deliver maximum effort each time, win, lose or draw. Even if things don't go well on a given weekend as far as the final results are concerned, you can still be 100 percent successful if your personal yardstick is calibrated this way. It's up to you. It's your choice and choice can be the greatest power you have, whether you are an elite athlete, a corporate leader or a family leader.

Focus on the process, not the prize—the process of personal excellence in the moment, bringing the best you've got to everything you do. Enjoy the process—take the time on a regular basis to stop and sniff the flowers along the way—and be satisfied that whatever the result, you've done your part to the fullest. That is the hallmark of the true champion.

I have really enjoyed putting my thoughts down on paper for a second time and I hope you have found the stories and analogies both interesting and informative. I learned a lot about what I have written by recognizing my own weaknesses and consequently looking deeper into the makeup of the great champions. My hope is, and indeed my whole reason for writing this second edition book, is to make you think a little more. To make you a little more aware of what might be just around the corner, and to give you the ability to take a correct step you might not have been able to take by yourself. However, always remember we are all individuals with unique qualities. Use the information given to supplement and stretch your own personhood. Do not use the information to try to become someone you are not. Stay true to yourself and enjoy the success. There will be joy in the journey, and I will enjoy seeing some of you on the podium.

Best wishes,
Derek Daly
Derek Daly Academy

APPENDIX

PITFIT

PITFIT TRAINING is the recognized leader in developing driver specific fitness, nutrition and human performance programs to the expressly address the physical and mental demands of the motorsports industry.

PitFit was founded in 1997 by Jim Leo. Leo and the PitFit crew provide fitness training to racers and various series from karts to cars. With the addition of numerous experts in the field of biomechanics, exercise physiology, rehabilitation, nutrition and mental training, the PitFit Training program covers the primary areas needed for motorsports human performance. The key element of variety in training options relies heavily on top experts in the areas of boxing, yoga, mixed martial arts, swimming, rock climbing, triathlon and many more offerings.

In January 2010, PitFit Training opened its new facility in Indianapolis that housed experts in chiropractic medicine, physical therapy, rehabilitation and massage along with a training center filled with the many tools used to train drivers of all levels.

The roster of champions that have become part of the PitFit family is literally a who's who of auto racing. Drivers such as Scott Dixon, Dario Franchitti, Will Power, Kasey Kahne, Sam Hornish Jr., Larry Dixon, Morgan Lucas, Levi Jones and Justin Allagier are just a few of the many drivers who have trained with PitFit.

PitFit Training has become literally its own ladder system for racing success, with numerous drivers starting in the program in lower-level series and staying with the training as they graduate to the top levels. In 2011, six former Firestone Indy Lights drivers from the PitFit program moved up to the Izod IndyCar Series. They were Wade Cunningham, J.R. Hildebrand, James Hinchcliffe, Pippa Mann, Sebastian Saavedra and Charlie Kimball.

Ultimately, PitFit Training has grown into the industry leader in the development and implementation of motorsports-specific human performance training and lists clients from Formula One, IndyCar, NASCAR, NHRA, Grand-Am, ALMS, USAC and numerous junior level auto racing series.

To schedule an interview, contact Jim Leo at 317-388-1000 or jleo@pitfit.com. To learn more, visit www.pitfit.com.

PERFORMANCE PRIME

In early 1984, Dr. Jacques Dallaire was joined in his efforts by colleague and friend Dr. Dan Marisi, a sport and educational psychology specialist, and the program the two scientists developed over the years expanded to include mental skills evaluation and training in addition to the physiology component. Dr. Marisi played a key role with Dr. Dallaire in the development and delivery of the performance enhancement activities that ultimately became known around the world as the human performance international (HPI) program.

In late 1984, Dr. Dallaire was recruited by the then director general of Sport Canada, Ms. Abby Hoffman, and the president of the Canadian Association of Sport Sciences to become the manager of science and medicine programs at Sport Canada, a major department within the Canadian Government's Ministry of Fitness and Amateur Sport. In this post, Dr. Dallaire served as the primary coordinator of the science and medicine support initiatives aimed at the more than 70 Canadian national sport governing bodies as well as the direct liaison between the Canadian federal government and the Sport Medicine Council of Canada and its member agencies.

In 1992, Drs. Dallaire and Marisi relocated to the Daytona Beach area to tackle the continued development and delivery of their performance programs on a full-time basis. While the sport of motor racing represented the lion's share of their early clientele, the HPI program also welcomed athletes from other sports as well as various high-performance occupational professionals. The program continued to evolve and in late 1998, the duo decided to move the company to the Charlotte, NC, area, where it continues to operate today.

Since the untimely passing of Dr. Marisi in 1999, the primary responsibility for program development and delivery has fallen to Dr. Dallaire. In 2005, he became the primary consultant and chief scientist for Dallaire Consulting LLC (parent company to Performance Prime), an organization that was founded to further expand his performance enhancement activities in the corporate environment and beyond. The company's mission has broadened and today, Dr. Dallaire's activities include program and product development that extends beyond the world of sport to include high-performance corporate and occupational domains, as well as the field of rehabilitation.

Over the past 40 years, Dr. Dallaire has been exposed to the application of a great many sport science and medicine strategies and techniques within the high-performance sport world and has been in an excellent position to monitor what has been effective and what has not. Over this time, he has refined his understanding of what is missing in the performance enhancement equation and continues to focus on addressing these perceived needs.

To schedule an appointment call Dr. Dallaire at 704-699-1725 or info@performanceprime.com. To learn more, visit www.performanceprime.com.

ST. VINCENT SPORTS PERFORMANCE

St. Vincent Sports Performance is the largest hospital-based sports medicine program in the stare of Indiana.

Whether you play basketball for fun, pound the pavement for marathon runs or have a mean overhand tennis serve, you don't want to be sidelined with an injury. But injuries do happen. And when they do, St.Vincent sports medicine physicians are ready to help you get back in the game, with the largest hospital-based sports medicine program in Indiana. St.Vincent offers a full range of physical therapy services for sports-specific injuries in our hospitals, outpatient clinics and specialty clinics. Sports medicine services are offered at St.Vincent Anderson Regional Hospital in Anderson through the Carl D. Erskine Rehabilitation Center.

St.Vincent Sports Performance is a medically based program with a wide variety of offerings. We are not just about performance—jumping higher, going faster— although that's a big part of what we do. Our philosophy focuses on injury prevention and injury management. We understand the demands of athletics, so we:

- Identify weaknesses, including problems from previous injuries that affect performance
- Assess and identify problems
- Provide a wide range of guidance, including physician referrals when needed

We offer benefits to all types of athletes in central Indiana—from recreational sports enthusiasts to youth athletes to professionals, including world class Olympians, Indy 500 champions, NFL and NBA players. With more than a century of combined experience in getting the most from an athlete's potential, we help athletes of all ages and abilities gain a competitive edge.

To schedule an appointment call 317-415-5747 or toll free at 800-277-8817. To learn more visit, www.stvincent. org/Sports-Medicine-and-Sports-Performance

DRIVING SCHOOLS

Driving schools are a very good resource for the parents and others as part of the development of a driver. Here is a list of some good racing schools:

BERTIL ROOS RACING SCHOOL

As a pioneer in the industry, the Bertil Roos Racing School has been training students in the art of motor racing for over a quarter of a century. Graduates of our school can be found at every level of racing, from the hobbyist up to the top levels of professional racing.

Bertil Roos Racing School

P.O. Box 221, Route 115

Blakeslee, PA 18610

(800) 722-3669

(570) 646-7227

customerservice@bertilroos.com

BONDURANT RACING SCHOOL

We want you to be a better driver. It sounds simple enough, but the Bob Bondurant School of High Performance Driving has pulled out all the stops to get you there. Everything we do is geared toward instilling The Bondurant Method within you. In order to promote our method, we push ourselves to bring you the best of everything—the finest facility, the most up-to-date cars and equipment, the most qualified staff, the best training methods, and the highest standards in order to help you reach your goals—whatever they may be.

Bondurant Racing School

20000 S. Maricopa Road,

Gate #3 in Chandler, Arizona 85226

(800) 842-7223

www.bondurant.com

BRIDGESTONE RACING ACADEMY

Our top trainers are full-time dedicated teaching professionals. Add a crew of 19 race mechanics, plus four office administrators, plus two instructors and that's at least 26 people per day to serve a class of twelve students. Toss in a few corner workers, the lunch chef and the ambulance workers who come and go and it's little wonder that we have *never* been told that other schools exceed our high level of service—ever!

Bridgestone Racing Academy

Box 373

Pontypool, ON L0A1K0 Canada

(905) 983-1114

www.race2000.com

SIMRACEWAY PERFORMANCE DRIVING CENTER

In 1957, British racing champion Jim Russell founded the racing school industry and realized his dream of teaching people from all walks of life the fine art of motor racing. His school was the world's first training facility for racing drivers. The school, now called the Simraceway Performance Driving Center, graduates hundreds of career-minded racers in addition to thousands of motoring enthusiasts each year, taking with them the experience of a lifetime.

Simraceway Performance Driving Center Campus

Turn 1, Sonoma Raceway

29359 Arnold Drive Sonoma, CA 95476

(800) 733-0345

(707) 939-7600

pdc_info@simraceway.com

SKIP BARBER RACING SCHOOL LLC

Since 1975, Skip Barber has operated a fully integrated system of racing schools, driving schools, racing championships, corporate events and special projects across North America. No other organization delivers such a combination of high quality instruction, equipment, facilities and memorable experiences.

Skip Barber Racing School LLC

5290 Winder Hwy.

Braselton, GA 30517

(800) 221-1131

sales@skipbarber.com

INDEX